WONDERS of the SKY

WONDERS
of the
SKY

Tamra Andrews

Wonders of Nature: Natural Phenomena in Science and Myth

A Member of the Greenwood Publishing Group

Westport, Connecticut • London

Library of Congress Cataloging-in-Publication Data

Andrews, Tamra, 1959–
    Wonders of the sky / Tamra Andrews.
        p.   cm.—(Wonders of nature)
    Includes bibliographical references and index.
    ISBN 1–59158–104–4 (alk. paper)
        1. Astronomy—Popular works.   I. Title.   II. Wonders of nature (Libraries
    Unlimited)
    QB44.3.A59   2004
    520—dc22   2003065654

British Library Cataloguing in Publication Data is available.

Library of Congress Catalog Card Number: 2003065654
ISBN: 1–59158–104–4

First published in 2004

Libraries Unlimited, 88 Post Road West, Westport, CT 06881
A Member of the Greenwood Publishing Group, Inc.
www.lu.com

Printed in the United States of America

The paper used in this book complies with the
Permanent Paper Standard issued by the National
Information Standards Organization (Z39.48–1984).

10 9 8 7 6 5 4 3 2 1

Contents

CONTENTS

Illustrations

Preface

Teachers' guides are abundant in the area of astronomy, and lesson plans and activities are easily accessible on-line. But this is a different kind of astronomy guide; it combines science with myth, and it stresses how human curiosity shaped the history of science as ancient people learned to recognize patterns in the sky. Ancient myths contain a vivid imagery of the celestial world, with powerful sky gods who glide through the heavens and keep the world moving in continuing cycles. In this book, chapters on the Sun, Moon, stars, planets, and our Milky Way galaxy center on beliefs that arose as people recognized the rhythms of the heavens. Chapters on comets, meteors, and eclipses center on beliefs that arose when people witnessed an eruption of those rhythms.

Wonders of the Sky was born from years of fascination with sky legends and from a recognition that myth and science are intricately entwined. In examining the sky myths of different cultures, we can see that people have always had a desire to interpret nature's messages, and the myths and legends that arose from this desire served as an early form of philosophy. Each chapter in this teachers' guide contains an adaptation of a sky myth and an explanation of the science behind the myth. Topics for discussion and projects should be useful for lessons in art and creative writing, and they center as much on the culture that told the myth as on the science behind it.

The proliferation of books and Web sites that contain information on astronomy and culture made selection of reference sources difficult, so I limited the list of teacher resources in the appendix to books that were particularly helpful in preparing this guide and to general Web sites that contain grade-appropriate explanations, lessons, and projects or collections of astronomical myths. In each chapter I have included books and Web sites that should help students complete the projects and a list of additional sources to help teachers guide class discussions. Annotations appear with the citations.

Much of this material was gathered while doing research for my encyclopedia of nature myths, entitled *Legends of the Earth, Sea, and Sky: An Encyclopedia of Nature Myths* (Santa Barbara, CA: ABC-CLIO, 1998). This book can be found in many school and public libraries, and the paperback edition, published under the name *Dictionary of Nature Myths: Legends of the Earth, Sea, and Sky* (New York: Oxford University Press, 2000), is available in bookstores. Neither this teachers' guide nor my encyclopedia would be possible were it not for Dr. E. C. Krupp of the Griffith Observatory in Los Angeles, Dr. R. Robert Robbins of the University of Texas at Austin, and the many other scholars whose works I relied on for information. Dr. Krupp's book, *Beyond the Blue Horizon: Myths and Legends of the Sun, Moon, Stars, and Planets* (New York: Oxford University Press, 1991), proved to be an invaluable source of information, as did the educational articles and resources that appear on the Stardate Web site produced by McDonald Observatory (http://stardate.org) and on many of the other Web sites listed in the Teacher Resources appendix. Dr. Krupp's book provides insight into numerous astronomical myths and clear explanations for all the astronomical phenomena covered in this guide.

I'd like to particularly thank my daughter Cristen Andrews for her help in preparing this guide. Cristen is a photojournalism major at the University of Texas at Austin, and she created the graphics that accompany this text. Her dedication and support mean the world to me. I'd like to thank Tim Jones and Stardate for the use of the four constellation graphics in Chapter 3. I'd also like to thank Frank Fox, a librarian at Texas State University, for helping me with research. I'd like to thank Sharon Coatney, my editor at Libraries Unlimited, for her support and encouragement.

It is my hope that teachers will find this guide useful not only for science lessons, but also for lessons in social studies, literature, and art. It is also my hope that students who read these myths and learn the science within them will gain an understanding of nature's clockwork, an appreciation of nature's power, and a recognition that people of all cultures and at all times in history shared the human desire to interpret the world around them. From this desire, science was born.

Introduction

Long ago, when no city lights obstructed the heavens, the phenomena of the night sky looked spectacular. It's hard for most of us to imagine a sky so dark that the stars overpower the night and the Milky Way cuts through the heavens as a band of glistening light. The myths help us imagine what it was like. People told these myths long ago to explain what they saw when they gazed into the night. They saw a magical world sparkling above them and they imagined that supernatural beings were responsible for the magic they saw. Ancient people invested these beings with the power to set patterns and order the world—and with the power to disrupt the order and cause destruction.

The people who told these sky myths long ago tried to make sense of events they witnessed in the heavens that scientists today understand as scientific phenomena. Ancient mythmakers invested the Sun and the Moon and the other celestial bodies with the same qualities they knew in themselves. Movement meant life. So when early people saw the Sun and the Moon move in the sky just as they themselves moved on Earth, they believed that the Sun and the Moon acted by force of will. People who knew nothing of science saw the Sun rise and believed that only a powerful god could light the world. They saw the Moon fade away to nothing and then return to a full, round ball, and they believed that only an immortal goddess could die and return to life. They also saw how the powerful gods and the immortal goddesses of the sky set patterns that influenced events on Earth. Patterns of light in the heavens looked like supernatural animals, and when certain animals rose into the sky, the seasons changed.

Early people may not have understood the science of astronomy, but in their attempt to make sense of the world, they came to understand. Supernatural power inspired both awe and fear, and so people had a driving need to make sense of what they saw in the world above them. Early people watched the sky closely and they used myth and storytelling to record their observations. People all over the world created sky myths to document not only the physical movements they witnessed, but also the religious beliefs that permeated their culture.

It's amazing to read these myths today and compare the sky knowledge ancient people learned by simply watching the sky with the sky knowledge modern astronomers have learned through scientific method. It's amazing to learn that people in societies all over the world created similar myths because people everywhere have similar needs and fears. We look at the sunrise today and call it science and we look at the stars in the night sky and have a difficult time recognizing the gods and animals early people saw there. But people everywhere, in ancient times and today, want to believe in miracles. Read the myths and you'll come to recognize the science of the sky as miracles. Learn the science behind the myths and you'll come to understand how the human desire to unravel the mysteries of the night sky led people to use their eyes and their minds to build a world of knowledge about our physical universe.

1 ⋯⋯⋯⋯⋯⋯⋯⋯⋯⋯⋯⋯⋯⋯⋯⋯ The Sun

THE MYTHS OF THE SUN

When ancient people witnessed the rising and setting Sun, they recognized order in the world. People long ago depended on the rhythms of the sky, and the cycle of the Sun affirmed the existence of a continuing, reliable rhythm. The Sun rose every day in the east, ascended to its highest point at midday, and set every day in the west. Then it rose again. But when the Sun set, the darkness seemed threatening. Early people attributed the Sun's movement to a powerful sky god, and when they watched their god disappear underneath the Earth, their source of light and heat disappeared as well. The Sun god had to rise again to renew the world, and the people could only imagine the terrors that might prevent him from doing so.

Because early people relied on the Sun god to sustain life, myths of solar movement featured the Sun god as a cosmic hero. Like all heroes, he had battles to fight and he had enemies to conquer, and life on Earth depended on whether or not the Sun god won the battles. The people knew that he had the power to win, because he rose every day and lit the world. But they also knew that the darkness demons waged a tough war. Sometimes, the demons succeeded in suppressing the Sun's power so thoroughly that clouds covered the sky. Sometimes they swallowed the Sun completely, in what we now call an eclipse.

The following myth was told by ancient Egyptians who worshipped the Sun as the highest power in existence. Many other groups of people worshipped the Sun, but the Egyptians made the Sun god their creator and attached primary significance to his journey across the heavens.

Read the myth below and discuss how it reflects early beliefs about the Sun and solar movement. Then use The Science of the Sun section to explain solar facts. A list of topics for discussion and projects appears at the end of the chapter.

"Ra's Perilous Journey," a Myth from Egypt

On a hilltop in a vast desert land, ancient worshippers gathered together and prayed for the sunrise. They prayed to Ra, their creator god and the greatest power in existence, falcon head of Heliopolis, the City of the Sun. It was Ra's job to rise every day above the horizon in the east and light the world, and it was Ra's job to turn the seasons and guarantee continued life for the world.

Ra had a journey to make each day, and the people of Egypt knew it was a dangerous one. Each day Ra boarded his solar boat and set sail across the river of heaven. Then, each night he sunk below the horizon in the west and faced the Powers of Darkness. The people of Egypt watched Ra sink below the horizon, where he abandoned his day boat and boarded a night boat, the Barque of a Million Years, which carried him into the realm of death. This was the land where Apep, the serpent, ruled. Each night Apep emerged from the river of darkness and attempted to swallow Ra and his boat. But Ra fought the great serpent demon, attacking him with spears. Each night, as Ra's spears pierced the scaly body of Apep, the sky over Egypt turned red with the demon's blood.

Ra battled Apep and his demon forces for twelve long hours each night, and if the Sun god won, he rose above the horizon in the east the next day and lit the world. So the people praised him. Fortunately, Ra always emerged triumphant. Renewed after his nightly battles, the Sun shone once again over Egypt, and the world continued.

Ra ruled as the great sky god of Egypt from the beginning of time. He created himself from the water and then he created all the other gods who ruled beneath him. In the beginning, the universe was only water. It was a great primordial ocean, and from it, all form and substance emerged. Ra emerged from this primordial ocean. He created Shu and Tefnut, the gods of air and moisture. Then, from the union of Shu and Tefnut, Geb and Nut arose. Geb was the god of Earth and Nut was the goddess of sky, and together they created Isis, Osiris, Seth, and Nephthys. These eight gods formed the Ennead, the primary gods of Heliopolis, and Ra ruled them all. Then Ra pushed Geb and Nut apart, making the sky and the Earth separate realms. Many other gods came into existence later but they all arose from Ra. Then Ra created human beings from his tears. And the people worshipped him.

"Praise, Ra," the people chanted. "Praise the Creator, Lord of the Sky." They praised their creator Sun in many forms. "Praise Khepri," the people cried. "Praise Khepri, the Scarab Beetle who renews the world."

The worshippers in Heliopolis gathered in temples and on hilltops and prayed that Ra continue to rule supreme and continue to dispel the evil powers that threaten the world. They watched the sky darken as Ra sunk beneath the western horizon, and they prayed that he would travel safely through the realm of the dead. They prayed that he destroy Apep, the demon serpent. Apep slithered through the waters beneath the Earth, waiting to annihilate the Sun god.

Ra faced his archenemy Apep every night and entered into battle with him and his army of serpent demons. Apep was enormous, and he thrust his massive body through the waters of the celestial Nile and up to the surface where he attacked Ra and his boat. Apep's army of serpents helped him. They guarded the gates to the Underworld and they slithered through deep, dark waters that ran through caverns beyond the gates. Ra sailed the water skillfully, however, through twelve caverns, flooding each one with light and dispelling the demons of darkness within them. Fortunately, Ra had help fighting the demons. An army of powerful gods accompanied him on his journey in the solar barque. A ram-headed Ra took the helm, and the other gods helped keep the boat on course. Lady of the Boat, a goddess wearing cow horns and a sun disk, sat among them. Two gods sat at the prow and four gods steered the oars. Two sets of nine baboons accompanied Ra too, as did twelve serpent goddesses and a host of other deities. The solar boat that carried them was golden and shaped like a crescent, and the people of Egypt watched the boat sink below Manu, the western mountain. Darkness engulfed the land.

The people could only imagine the terrors Ra and his crew faced in the land below the horizon, and they uttered prayers and chants to help guide their Sun god through the underworld caverns. His crew helped guide him as well. The baboons on Ra's boat opened the doors to the Underworld and sang to the Sun god as he entered, and the serpent goddesses lit up the darkness. Ra entered the first cavern chanting the secret names of deities who guarded this dangerous realm, and by doing this he warded off their attacks.

"Stinger, Frightener—submit," he chanted. "Fearful Visage of your cavern. Hand over the souls of this place of destruction."

Sailing through the First Cavern of Duat, the Egyptian Underworld, Ra faced the prisoners and he greeted the gods in their coffins. Ra sailed through the Second Cavern, and the Third. Fire-spitting cobras emerged from their lake of fire and flames licked at Ra's boat. Ra and his crew sailed past hordes of demons in the caverns, some with heads that faced backwards and others with the bodies of humans and the heads of animals, torches, or knives. He sailed through a slanted passageway with two doors guarded by snakes, and he entered the Fifth Cavern and Hall of Osiris. Osiris was god of the dead and the ruler of Duat, and he sat enthroned in this cavern holding a crook, the symbol of power, and an ankh, the symbol of life. Ra sailed through the Sixth Cavern, and then the Seventh and Eighth, facing danger all the way. In the Ninth Cavern Apep heaved his massive body up from the celestial Nile to the surface of the water and lay in the Sun god's path. Apep was a picture of destruction. He had no ears, no nose, and no eyes, and he whirled through the darkness breathing roars of terror.

Ra's boat sailed into the Ninth Cavern. Apep lunged from the water. But Ra and the powers of light bound Apep with ropes. The monster succumbed to the Sun god's power. He sunk below the water.

Ra survived his perilous journey and defeated the forces of chaos, but the people of Egypt continued to pray to the Sun and waited to see him rise victorious above Bahku, the eastern mountain. Ra remained in the Underworld until a day boat emerged from the celestial waters to carry him the rest of the way, through the last caverns of darkness. The heroic Ra boarded the boat and a swallow perched on the prow to announce the Sun's emergence in the sky.

Then, energized from his journey and transformed into Khepri, the golden scarab, the all-powerful Ra broke through the desert sand. The sun disk appeared in the Egyptian sky and flooded the world with light.

"Praise Ra," the people rejoiced. "Praise the all-powerful Sun, the renewer of life."

The sun cult of Egypt had its center in Heliopolis, the City of the Sun, but the worship of Ra extended throughout the land and entered into the rituals of every cult. The Sun god was a cosmic hero. He fought the forces of evil every night and won. Ra's perilous sky journey turned day to night and night to day, and it moved the Earth through the cycle of seasons. So the Sun god ruled and he ruled supreme—for as long as the people of Egypt praised him, and as long as he continued to renew the world.

This account of Ra's journey through the heavens was adapted from descriptions of the original myth as it appeared in the *Book of Caverns*, the *Book of Gates*, and the *Book of Am-Duat*, or the *Book of What Is in the Underworld*, and from explanations of these ancient compilations that appear in George Hart's *Egyptian Myths* (Austin: University of Texas Press, 1990).

THE SCIENCE OF THE SUN

"Ra's Perilous Journey" is a myth that explains the Sun's movement across the sky and the phenomena of day and night. It reflects an ancient knowledge of cosmic order and it affirms the importance of the forces of Sun and river that shaped Egyptian life. It also reveals a recognition of patterns and cycles that served as the basis for calendars. Ra had the responsibility for moving time forward, and the development of clocks and calendars arose from the knowledge of his solar myth.

BELIEF: The Sun is a powerful source of light and heat that sustains life on Earth.

The Sun is certainly a powerful source of light and heat and it does sustain life on Earth, but it is also an ordinary star. Ancient people could not have recognized the Sun as an ordinary star because from Earth it looks nothing like a star. It looks much bigger and brighter because it's so close to Earth. The Sun is 93.2 million miles away from

Earth, whereas the next closest star, Proxima Centauri, is 300,000 times farther away than that. Once scientists understood that the Sun was a star, they could learn about the structure and evolution of other stars that are much farther away than the Sun and much more difficult to study.

Look at the diagram of the Sun's atmosphere shown in Figure 1.1. The Sun is so hot and so bright because it's composed of layer upon layer of hot gases. These gases get denser and denser as they get closer to the Sun's core. The brightest part of the Sun is called the *photosphere*, and the temperature in the photosphere varies from close to 8,000 degrees to over 10,000 degrees Fahrenheit. Outside the photosphere is the *chromosphere* and above that is the *corona*. The photosphere, chromosphere, and corona make up the Sun's atmosphere, and the photosphere is what you see shining brightly in the sky. In fact, the photosphere shines so brightly that skywatchers can only see the chromosphere and the corona during a solar eclipse.

FIGURE 1.1 · The Sun's Atmosphere

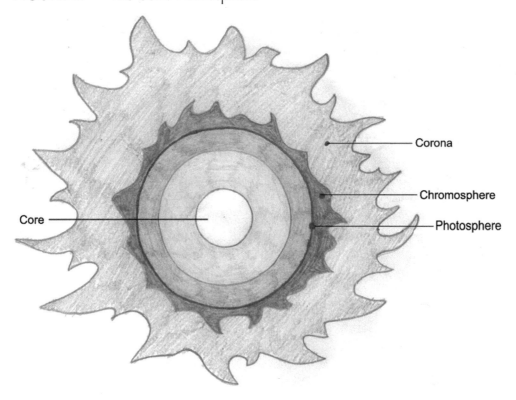

Core

Corona

Chromosphere

Photosphere

BELIEF: The Sun rises in the east, moves across the sky, and sets in the west.

Sun gods in myths all over the world made daily journeys across the heavens, and ancient people relied on the movement of the Sun to keep the world turning. However, the Sun only appears to move across the sky. Astronomers call this the "apparent motion" of the Sun. It only moves across the sky because the Earth rotates on its axis. It rotates from east to west, and it rotates a full circle in 24 hours. The Earth's rotation on its axis makes the Sun appear brightest at midday when it rises to zenith, the point due north of the observer. This is when Ra appeared to the people in the prime of his life. As the Sun god moved, he aged, and he changed forms in the process. He appeared to rise above the eastern horizon as a scarab beetle, and he appeared to sink below the western horizon as an old man. In reality, however, the Sun makes no journey across the sky at all; the Earth is turning all by itself.

BELIEF: Ra travels through a river in the sky.

The concept of the celestial Nile stemmed from the concept that the Earth mirrored the heavens. It stemmed from the concept of cosmic order, the idea that the sky was a model of order and the sky gods set patterns for the people on Earth to follow. Because the sky was the model of order, the people imagined the celestial sphere as a world much like their own. In Egypt the Nile River defined the land, so the Egyptian heaven contained a celestial Nile, and so did the Egyptian underworld. The river that flowed through the sky and the underworld held creatures similar to the creatures that inhabited the rivers on Earth. The dangerous Nile crocodile inhabited the earthly waters, and Apep lived in the celestial Nile. The desert also defined the land of Egypt, and Apep's army of night serpents inhabited the underworld just as perilous snakes lived beneath the desert sand.

In "Ra's Perilous Journey," the Sun god traveled the heavens in a boat, or a barque. This reflects how the people of Egypt themselves traveled. In myths from Greece, the Sun god rode a chariot across the heavens. In myths of North America and Australia, he traveled on foot. Myth is an expression of life, and the elements within a myth reflect the mythmaker's knowledge of the world. The people of Egypt traveled along the Nile River, so it made sense to them that the gods traveled along a counterpart to the Nile River in the sky.

Ra had two boats, one that took him through twelve stations of day and one that took him through twelve stations of night. His day boat carried him from the eastern horizon to the west, and his night boat carried him from the western horizon underneath the Earth. Water flowed both above the horizon and below it. The belief that water existed in heaven stemmed from the perception of water as infinite, and it appeared in the myths of many cultures. The sea seemed to disappear below the horizon, but in ancient thought, the horizon extended into the sky. Celestial rivers characterized the sky myths of other people who also lived in lands dominated by water sources. Indian myths tell of the celestial Ganges and Chinese myths tell of the celestial Tien Ho, or Silver River. Peruvian myths tell of the celestial Vilacanota River, which plays a crucial role in the water cycle. You'll read more about the Vilacanota River in the chapter on the Milky Way, and you'll learn that many early people perceived the Milky Way as a river in the sky.

BELIEF: The Sun travels through twelve stations of day and twelve stations of night.

Ra's sky journey takes him through twelve stations of day and twelve stations of night because Egypt is close to the equator, where the days and nights are nearly equal. The Egyptians were the first to divide the day into 24 hours, and they developed an accurate calendar based on the motions of the Sun as early as 4200 B.C. People learned to make calendars based on the motions of the Moon first, possibly as early as the ice age. The Egyptian solar calendar was more accurate than the lunar calendars, however, and it was adopted by other cultures and used as an astronomical reference throughout the Middle Ages.

It's quite remarkable that the ancient Egyptians had no knowledge of the Earth's rotation and yet they developed a calendar based on solar movement. They began their day at dawn when Ra rose above the eastern horizon, and they began their night at dusk when he sunk below the horizon in the west. Calendar makers of other societies began their day at dusk or at midnight, like we do today.

The Egyptians based their calendar on the motions of the Sun, but also on the motions of Sirius, the brightest star in the night sky. Sirius really isn't that bright compared to the other stars, but it appears bright because it's so close to Earth. People all over the world used Sirius as a seasonal marker. The Egyptians marked the beginning of each new year by the star's first appearance in the sky just before dawn. By co-incidence, the first appearance of Sirius occurred just before the annual flood of the Nile. Therefore, the ancient Egyptians assigned Sirius special significance. In Egypt, the annual flood was essential for fertilizing the Nile river valley, and because the Egyptians believed that Sirius caused the flood they believed that the star brought fertility to the Earth. They identified Sirius with the goddess Isis. Isis, like Ra, renewed the world, and both of these deities served as timekeepers. The Egyptians split their calendar year into twelve months, each with thirty days and five additional festival days. This made a year of 365 days. This worked for a while, but eventually the Egyptian calendar fell out of use. A year is really a few hours more than 365 days, and we compensate for those extra hours today by adding an extra day during leap year. The ancient Egyptians simply kept time by the risings of Ra and of Isis, two powerful gods of the sky.

BELIEF: The Sun moves the seasons.

Just as the Sun only appears to move across the sky because the Earth rotates on its axis, the Sun only appears to move the seasons because the Earth revolves around the Sun. As the Earth revolves, it tilts on its axis 23½ degrees. This is another "apparent motion" of the Sun. Early people didn't know this, but because they tracked the Sun's movement so closely they noticed that it appeared to rise and set at different places as the year progressed. They gave their Sun god credit for turning the seasons because they watched him rise a little farther to the north as the Earth got colder and winter came. Then they watched him change course and rise a little farther to the south as the Earth got warmer and summer returned. People of the ancient world watched the behavior of the other celestial bodies in the universe, but they had no recognition of their own place in the solar system and how it affected the movement of the heavens. The Sun brought light to the world every day, and the Sun brought warmth to the world every summer.

Sun gods held such high places in ancient myths because people knew the importance of returning warmth to the Earth. People all over the world assigned special significance to the solstices, the two days of the year when the Sun appeared to reach the farthest point on his northward or southward journey. The word *solstice* derives from Latin and means "sun stand still," and on two days of the year the Sun does appear to stand still. On the winter solstice the Sun stops moving south and turns around to head north, and on the summer solstice the Sun stops moving north and turns around to head south again. The Sun doesn't really stop of course, but the Sun appears to stop because it slows down as the year approaches the solstices. Observers long ago could not detect any solar movement for five or six days in a row. It seemed to early skywatchers that the Sun god paused in his journey across the heavens, as if he had to make up his mind whether to turn around or keep right on going in the same direction. To ancient people who perceived the Sun as a supernatural being with a will of his own, the solstices were frightening times.

What if the Sun god decided not to turn? He had to keep going to continue the cycle of seasons. So people in ancient cultures all over the world decided to do what they could to make sure the Sun turned around. They held solstice ceremonies in hopes that they could influence the Sun's behavior. Winter solstice ceremonies held more crucial significance than the summer ceremonies and therefore involved elaborate rituals. That's because the people had watched their Earth grow cold and their fields die during the winter, and they knew the Sun had to turn north in order to renew warmth and light to the world. Figure 1.2 shows how the Sun's apparent motion changes the seasons on Earth.

FIGURE 1.2 · The Seasons

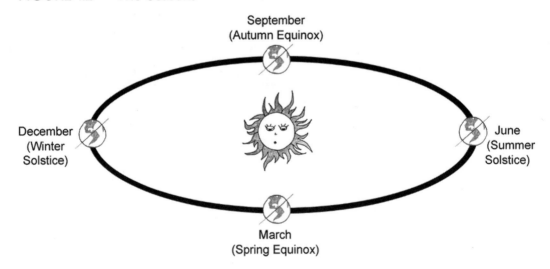

BELIEF: The Sun god is a cosmic hero who
maintains order in the world.

The alteration between darkness and light is one of nature's most obvious rhythms. The change between the two served as a basis for clocks and calendars and helped make sense of the world. In the myths, gods of light fought constant battles against demons of darkness. These fights symbolized the eternal battle between good and evil, and when Sun gods fought these battles and won, they achieved victory for the world. The notion of a heroic Sun god was so pervasive that many of the world's myths have been interpreted as solar myths and many of the world's gods have been identified as solar heroes. The Sun vanquished the darkness and restored order to the world.

In ancient Egypt, the pharaohs maintained order on Earth as the Sun gods did in heaven. Myths of kingship, in Egypt and in many other lands, often revolved around the belief in kings and pharaohs as direct descendents of the Sun god. In these countries, divine kingship was granted by solar power and based on the recognition of the Sun as an all-powerful god who ruled the world. The gods fought chaotic forces in the sky and the pharaohs fought chaotic forces on Earth, just as in "Ra's Perilous Journey" Ra fought Apep and his army of night serpents. From the time Ra separated the Earth from the sky, the pharaoh and the Sun god had to join forces. The Sun god could not maintain order on Earth once he separated from Earth and rose above it. So he endowed an earthly king with powers that enabled him to assume this function. In Egypt, the pharaoh became divine ruler and defender of the land.

— TOPICS FOR DISCUSSION AND PROJECTS

TOPIC 1. Sacred Animals of Egypt

In the myths of Ra, the Sun god appeared in different forms, usually as a man with the head of a ram, a hawk, or a falcon. This connection with the Sun god made these animals sacred, and the hawk, falcon, and many other animals were worshipped all over Egypt. The list below represents a selection of animals Egyptian mythmakers associated with astronomical objects. The Suggested Reading section, which follows the list, contains myths of the Egyptian gods. Read some of the myths about these animals and discuss how their attributes reflect early knowledge of the motions of the sky.

PROJECT IDEA

Have students make a mask of one of the animal-headed gods connected with a celestial object and talk about the significance of the animal in Egyptian myth. The list below represents animals the Egyptians associated with celestial bodies. The books in the Suggested Reading section contain myths of the animal-headed gods of Egypt as well as pictures that will help students design their masks.

Falcon, Hawk, and Other Birds—The falcon and the hawk were both connected to the Sun, and the Sun gods Horus and Ra both took the forms of men with falcon or hawk heads. Birds appeared in myths all over the world as symbols of celestial power, in part because their ability to fly allowed them access to the sky world. In Egyptian myth the hawk and the falcon served as solar symbols, and pictures of winged disks appeared all over the land to represent the Sun's power. Myths of Egypt and Greece both tell of a legendary bird called the phoenix that served as a symbol of fire and the Sun. The phoenix had feathers of red and gold. Because this legendary bird burned himself up but arose as a new bird from the ashes, the myth of the phoenix tells the story of the Sun's ability to renew itself.

Ram—The ram also served as a solar symbol and appeared in Egyptian myths as another symbol of Ra.

Cat—The Egyptian Moon goddess Bast surfaced in the myths as a woman with a cat's head.

Lion—The Egyptians connected the lion with the rising and setting

Sun. They envisioned the Earth god Aker as two lions that guarded the Sun as it sunk below the western horizon and entered the underworld and as it rose above the eastern horizon and emerged into the sky.

Cow—The cow symbolized both the Moon and the Sun in ancient Egypt, and the goddesses Hathor, Isis, and Nut were often depicted as cows.

Crocodile—The ancient Egyptians feared crocodiles because during times of drought they emerged from the water, wandered over the land, and devoured everything that lay in their path. The Egyptians identified the crocodile with the gods Set and Sebek, two demonic gods of death and destruction.

Scarab Beetle—Ra had different names and manifested himself in different forms. He appeared as Khepri, the scarab beetle, to symbolize solar movement and rebirth. When the Egyptians watched the scarab beetle roll its dung into a ball and push it along in front of him, they said that Khepri, the golden scarab, pushed the Sun across the sky. When they saw the beetle bury the dung in the ground and new beetles arise from it, they connected the scarab beetle to the Sun's disappearance in the west and its rebirth in the east.

Serpent or Snake—Myths surrounding the serpent demon Apep illustrate how Egyptian myths connected snakes with the demonic forces of the underworld. The early Egyptians often made wax models of Apep and burned them. They considered this a form of magic that would help insure that Ra would destroy Apep and renew the world each day.

SUGGESTED READING

Doney, Meryl. *Masks*. New York: Franklin Watts, 1997.

> Aimed at grades 4–6. Includes simple designs, color illustrations, and instructions for making masks from numerous cultures.

Sivin, Carole. *Maskmaking*. Worcester, MA: Davis, 1986.

> Gives instructions for making masks from various types of materials, including recycled materials, and includes a section on making masks with children.

Smith, A. G., and Hazen, Josie. *Cut and Make Egyptian Masks*. Mineola, NY: Dover, 1993.

> Has five masks to use for classroom decoration or for examples—King Tut, Lion, Falcon, Crocodile, and Jackal.

TOPIC 2. The Battle Between Darkness and Light, Order and Chaos

Sun gods like Ra had equivalents in every culture and they acted as superheroes in solar myths. Darkness demons often took the form of serpents or dragons that lurked beneath the Earth and suffered defeat each time the Sun rose in the sky. Fortunately for the world, the Sun god always slew the dragon. But the battle resumed each night. The god of light continually had to fight the demon of darkness because the alteration of darkness and night turned the world.

In the myth of Ra, the Sun created all in existence. Science has proven the Sun to be the originator of all life on Earth; without the Sun no vegetation could grow, and without the Sun the Earth could never revive from its winter death. Because of the significance of the Sun, scholars have interpreted many different kinds of stories as solar myths. Read some of the solar myths in the books listed below and compare the solar symbolism associated with the hero Sun god.

PROJECT IDEA

Have students make a poster depicting the battle between a Sun god and a demon of the darkness. Have them make the Sun god a superhero and the demon of darkness his nemesis. Have them identify the hero's superhuman powers and identify the power of his enemy. The poster should include a picture of the Sun god, a picture of his sidekicks, and a picture of the demon or demons he fights every day in his battle against darkness and chaos. Use the books below to identify common representations of Sun gods and night demons, and tell students to list characteristics of these supernatural beings on their poster. Have them include anything else they think will help place the characters they choose in a solar myth. They should give their hero a vehicle to carry him across the heavens and equip him with weapons of defense to help him fight the darkness and restore light to the world.

SUGGESTED READING

Ardagh, Philip. *Ancient Egyptian Myths and Legends*. Chicago: World Book, Inc., 2002.

> Contains retellings of Egyptian myths of gods and animals and explanations of the origins of these myths.

Budge, E. A. Wallis. *Egyptian Tales and Legends: Pagan, Christian, Muslim*. Mineola, NY: Dover, 2002.

Contains thirty-six myths and legends told by the well-known Egyptologist E. A. Wallis Budge.

TOPIC 3. Symbols of the Sun in Ancient Egypt

Because the ancient Egyptians worshipped the Sun, solar symbols permeated Egyptian myths. They decorated buildings and tombstones and they appeared in hieroglyphic documents that told the story of the Sun god's travels. The solar symbols in "Ra's Perilous Journey" include the hawk, the falcon, the ram, the cow, the ankh, the boat, and the scarab beetle. In other Egyptian myths, the Sun appeared as an all-seeing, all-knowing eye.

PROJECT IDEA

Have students create their own solar symbol based on what they have learned about the behavior of the Sun and the attributes of the Sun gods. The books below should help them identify symbols of the Sun used in myths from cultures around the world.

SUGGESTED READING

Bruce-Mitford, Miranda. *Illustrated Book of Signs and Symbols*. Mineola, NY: Dover, 1996.

> A reference book that contains color illustrations of signs and symbols in nature and in other subject areas. Includes symbols of the Sun.

Larson, Jennifer. *Egyptian Symbols: A Hieroglyphic Stamp Kit*. San Francisco: Chronicle Books, 2000.

> Contains twenty-nine large stamps with an explanation of Egyptian hieroglyphs and symbols and their cultural significance.

TOPIC 4. The Sun God and the Pharaoh

The people of Egypt worshipped their pharaoh as the Sun's descendent but also as an actual manifestation of the Sun god. The Inca believed their emperors descended from the Sun also, and so did the people of Japan and other people who worshipped their divine kings as solar deities. Believing that kings got their power from the Sun guaranteed the rulers' supremacy and affirmed their ability to keep the Earth in tune with the heavens. The Egyptian pharaoh had so much power that he himself ensured that the Sun moved safely through the heavens, and he ensured that the Sun renewed the world.

The connection between the Sun and the pharaoh is evidenced in three hieroglyphic compilations that detail Ra's journey; the *Book Am-Duat*, or the *Book of What Is in the Underworld*, the *Book of Gates*, and the *Book of Caverns*. Scenes from these books decorate the tombs of Rameses, and at one time solar artifacts filled the burial chambers. The tombs of the pharaohs constitute some of the greatest artifacts of ancient Egypt, and sadly, tomb robbers pillaged many of these ancient chambers and robbed the world of treasures that the Egyptians saw fit to bestow upon their divine rulers. For the most part, however, the scenes decorating the walls of these ancient tombs remain as a relic of an ancient culture with a rich history of solar worship.

PROJECT IDEA

Have students create a diorama or a model of a solar tomb that might be used for an Egyptian pharaoh. Tell them to use solar imagery to decorate the walls with a series of scenes that relate to Ra's travels through the underworld and his renewal on the eastern horizon. They might want to fill the inside of the tomb with solar artifacts. Egyptian tombs had multiple chambers, complete with trap doors and secret passageways and a deep shaft leading to a burial chamber. In many of these tombs the burial chamber lay deep underneath the ground and was considered a part of Duat, the Egyptian underworld. Have students place the most important artifacts in the burial chamber of their tomb, as the Egyptians did, to ensure that the deceased pharaoh has all that he needs when he arrives in the realm of the dead. The Egyptians believed that their pharaohs made the journey with Ra after they died and that placing amulets and solar symbols in their tombs helped the deceased conquer the demonic powers they would encounter in the underworld.

SUGGESTED READING

Applegate, Melissa Littlefield. *The Egyptian Book of Life: Symbolism of Ancient Egyptian Temple and Tomb Art*. Deerfield Beach, FL: HCI, 2001.

Written as a teachers' instruction manual, with color panels from temple and tomb wall paintings and lots of information on solar symbolism.

McDermott, Bridget. *Decoding Egyptian Hieroglyphs: How to Read the Secret Code of the Pharaohs*. San Francisco: Chronicle Books, 2001.

Contains colorful illustrations and photographs, a pronunciation and grammar guide, and maps, myths, and magic spells.

Reeves, C. N. *The Complete Valley of Kings: Tombs and Treasures of Egypt's Greatest Pharaohs*. New York: Thames and Hudson, 1996.

Contains illustrations of art and artifacts from the tombs of the pharaohs buried in the Valley of Kings, which has more than eighty tombs. Contains lots of details about the tombs and their treasures.

Shuter, Jane. *Pharaohs and Priests*. Chicago: Heinemann Library, 1999.

Discusses the role of pharaohs, priests, and numerous gods and goddesses of ancient Egypt and explains Egyptian death rituals.

Zuravicky, Orli. *Exploring Pyramids Around the World: Making Models of Geometric Solids*. New York: Powerkids Press, 2004.

To be released in 2004, this book covers the history and architecture of pyramids in different cultures and explains how to reconstruct them as models.

TOPIC 5. Solar Boats

Boats played a significant role in Egyptian myth and culture because the life of the early Egyptians revolved around the Nile River. Ra's Barque of a Million Years illustrates how the early Egyptians used boats for spiritual purposes. In Egyptian belief, it was not only Ra who made his sky journey in a boat, but also the pharaohs and even the common people. The dead pharaohs were thought to accompany Ra on his daily journey, and the souls of the dead were also said to accompany him on their journey to the afterlife.

PROJECT IDEA

Because the Egyptians believed the dead traveled through the celestial Nile with their Sun god, they included a boat in every tomb. Have students design a boat that might be buried in the tomb of an early Egyptian. They can use the sources below to get ideas on how to decorate their boats and they can view some of the elaborate boats that were designed for the Egyptian pharaohs.

SUGGESTED READING

Boats and Ships. Voyages of Discovery Series. New York: Scholastic, 1996.

> Contains colorful illustrations of boats and ships from around the world.

Roberts, Jerry. *The Amazing Book of Paper Boats*. San Francisco: Chronicle Books, 2001.

> Contains eighteen ready-to-assemble model boats and includes the history and folklore attached to them.

Smith, A. G. *Traditional Boats from Around the World*. Mineola, NY: Dover, 1983.

> Contains pictures of different types of boats used by people of many cultures.

TOPIC 6. Solar Clocks and Calendars

The ancient Egyptians noticed that the Sun rose and set, but they also noticed that it rose and set in a slightly different place every day. Early hunters noticed that it rose and set in certain places in the sky when the animals migrated to the hunting fields or when they went into hibernation for the winter. Early farmers noticed that it rose and set when the crops grew in the spring or when the fields froze in the winter. The point where the Sun rose and set changed with the seasons, and the understanding of this led to the development of solar clocks and calendars.

PROJECT IDEA

Have students make a sundial that early people might have used as a clock. The early Egyptians noticed that as the Sun moved, their shadows changed directions. So they built large sundials that they called *obelisks*. On the base they marked the twelve hours of Ra's journey. The sources below contain directions for making different kinds of sundials.

SUGGESTED READING

InternetWorks Ltd. "Sundials on the Internet." http://www.sundials.co.uk.

> Contains information on all aspects of sundials, including detailed instructions for projects, lists of books, and pictures of sundials.

Shapiro, Irwin I., Marvin Grossman, and R. Bruce Ward. *ARIES Exploring Time: Sundials, Water Clocks, and Pendulums: Science Journal.* Watertown, MA: Charlesbridge, 2000.

> Contains questions and activities to help students explore the concept of time and time measurement, and explains the history and use of numerous timekeeping instruments.

Skurzynski, Gloria. *On Time: From Seasons to Split Seconds.* Washington, DC: National Geographic Society, 2000.

> Presents an overview of the history of timekeeping, starting with the earliest attempts to make clocks and calendars. Discusses sundials, water clocks, atomic clocks, and wristwatches.

Trionfante, Jeffery V. *Sunclocks: Sundials to Make and Use.* Coos Bay, OR: JVT Publications, 1999.

> Includes the history of timekeeping, a useful glossary, and cutout sundials, as well as instructions for making your own sundial.

—— SUGGESTED READING FOR TEACHERS

In addition to the general sources listed in the Teacher Resources appendix of this guide, the following books will help you lead class discussions on Egyptian mythology. Some of the books listed are older books that may only be available in larger libraries, but they are standard sources on Egyptian mythology that you may find of interest. The Web sites listed in the Teacher Resources appendix contain information on solar astronomy as well as additional lessons and activities relating to the science of the sun.

Harris, Geraldine. *Gods and Pharaohs from Egyptian Mythology*. New York: Peter Bedrick Books, 1992.

> Contains adaptations of myths of Egypt and short stories suitable for classroom reading. Includes illustrations and a discussion of hieroglyphs.

Hart, George. *Egyptian Myths*. Austin: University of Texas Press, 1990.

> Contains an overview of Egyptian mythology, including a detailed explanation of Ra's journey through the heavens.

Hodge, Susie. *Ancient Egyptian Art*. Chicago: Heinemann Library, 1998.

> Award-winning book that explores the art of ancient Egypt, including wall paintings, reliefs, architecture, and sculpture. Puts art into historical context and shows how it relates to religious beliefs. Has full-color illustrations and a list of projects.

Krupp, E. C. *Beyond the Blue Horizon: Myths and Legends of the Sun, Moon, Stars, and Planets*. New York: Oxford University Press, 1991.

> A chapter entitled "From the Darkness" discusses Ra's journey through the heavens in length and includes other astronomical myths and facts about the Sun and solar movement.

Mercatante, Anthony S. *Zoo of the Gods: Animals in Myth, Legend and Fable*. New York: Harper & Row, 1974.

> Contains chapters on animals that appear in myths and legends all over the world. Each chapter contains information on how the animal appears in myths and on how and why it serves as a symbol. Chapters include "Animals of the Water," "Animals of the Earth," "Animals of the Air," and "Animals of the Mind."

O'Hara, Gwydion. *Sun Lore: Myths and Folklore from Around the World*. St. Paul, MN: Llewellyn, 1997.

> Contains solar myths from many lands, including Egypt, and an index of Sun gods.

Olcott, William Tyler. *Sun Lore of All Ages: A Survey of Solar Mythology, Folklore, Customs, Worship*. New York: Book Tree, 1999.

A survey of Sun myths from around the globe, including Egypt. Explains solar symbols and superstitions and elaborates on other cultural aspects, including ceremonies and festivals.

Quie, Sarah. *Myths and Civilization of the Ancient Egyptians*. New York: McGraw-Hill, 2001.

Uses myths to teach about the history, culture, and archaeology of ancient Egypt. Contains illustrations, maps, and diagrams.

Quirke, Stephen. *The Cult of Ra: Sun-Worship in Ancient Egypt*. London: Thames and Hudson, 2001.

Discusses the connection between the Sun god and the pharaohs of Egypt. Discusses the Sun god's role in creation, and the notion that all physical matter came from the Sun. Also discusses the importance of pyramids and obelisks in the Sun cult of ancient Egypt. Includes a discussion of Akhenaten.

Helpful Web Sites

In addition to many of the general Web sites listed in the Teacher Resources appendix, the following two sites are particularly helpful for studying the myths and science of the Sun.

Edgar, Robin. "The Total Solar Eclipse 'Web Sight.'" *http://totalsolareclipses.homestead.com/religion.html*.

Contains links to several good sites on the solar symbols in Egypt.

Stanford University. "Stanford Solar Center." *http://solar-center.stanford.edu*.

An excellent site that contains numerous innovative activities and lesson plans, solar folklore and art, a section where students can ask a solar astronomer questions about the Sun, and lots of scientific information about the Sun, including solar news and weather reports.

2 The Moon

THE MYTHS OF THE MOON

In myths all over the world the Moon represented change and immortality. The Moon changed from one form to another. It grew full and round, and then it shrunk down to nothing and disappeared. The Moon's ability to change was a remarkable thing, but it was even more remarkable that it appeared to die and resurrect. The changing Moon taught people when to plant and when to reap, and its ability to renew itself from death gave people the belief that the fields would grow again each spring after their apparent death each winter.

Lunar myths explained why the Moon waxed and waned and why it vanished from sight and appeared to die. Most myths made the Moon a beautiful goddess and they placed her in a silver sky palace and married her off to the Sun. People all over the world gazed at the Moon and tried to see the lovely goddess who lived there. Some people recognized her face in the patterns on the lunar surface, and some people recognized the images of animals they knew from the Earth realm and that lived in the Moon as well.

Read the following myth of Heng 'O, the illustrious Moon goddess from China. Heng 'O has been celebrated throughout history, and her myth holds significance even today as each year the Chinese people hold a harvest Moon festival to honor her. Discuss how this myth reflects early beliefs about the Moon. Then use The Science of the Moon section to explain the Moon's phases and to identify the features of the lunar surface that people recognized as their goddess.

"Heng 'O and Her Palace on the Moon," a Myth from China

On a cool, crisp autumn night, villagers from all over China gathered for the festival. They had come to honor Heng 'O, the illustrious Moon goddess who brought them light and life and a bountiful harvest. A shining crystal palace lit the sky with the magic of Moonlight. Below the sky the night air blew softly over the fields. Above the sky, Heng 'O danced on the Moon.

On that evening in autumn, women bustled about selling cakes and candies, and children held hands and ran about and played games in the moonlight. The air smelled of sugared fruit and spice cakes, and the women who had baked them wrapped woven shawls tightly around their children to keep them warm. The children danced in the moonlight, and they sang to the goddess they watched dancing above them. When the village storyteller called to the children, they ran eagerly to the hilltop and huddled together. They licked sugar from their lips and ran their toes through the soft, cool grass. The women stopped selling their sweets, and everyone sat in silence waiting. Then, when all was still, the storyteller began his tale. It was a tale that had been told to generations before, and a tale that would be told for generations to come. As the children listened intently, and as the sky filled with moonlight, the storyteller told of Heng 'O, their goddess, and how she came to live in the palace on the Moon.

"It was a long time ago," the storyteller began, "when gods and goddesses inhabited the world. It was a wonderful time, when magic existed everywhere. But it was also a dangerous time, for wherever gods and goddesses exist demons exist too, devils and monsters in all forms that blow tempests of wind and breathe fire from their mouths. Emperor Yao was afraid of these demons; he watched in horror as the winds swept over the fields and destroyed the crops, and he watched in horror as ten suns appeared in the sky and threatened to destroy the world. Emperor Yao knew that only one Sun ruled the sky, so he called his Divine Archer, Shen I, to shoot the nine false suns out of the sky before the strength of their heat killed everything in existence. Shen I answered the emperor's call."

The storyteller continued.

"Shen I was a mighty warrior, a defender of world order, and Heng 'O was his wife, the lovely sister of a water sprite. Shen I left his wife to fight for the world, and he traveled to the banks of the West River and climbed the mountain peaks where he discovered nine gigantic birds blowing anger from their mouths and forming balls of fire in the sky. Shen I loaded his bow and shot arrows at these demons. He pierced the birds' chests, and the nine suns dissolved into red clouds and disappeared. Like magic."

The children's eyes grew wide with wonder as the storyteller said those words. They knew about magic, and if any night were to bring them magic, this was the one.

"Emperor Yao rewarded Shen I grandly," the storyteller went on. "He rewarded the warrior with a pill that would make him immortal. Shen I took the pill back to his home and hid it in the rafters. Then he continued on his mission to destroy the demonic forces that threatened to lay waste to the land.

It was not long after Shen I left that Heng 'O noticed a brilliant light shining from the rooftop."

"Moonlight!" one of the children whispered audibly. Many had heard the story before.

"She climbed a ladder and chased after the light," the storyteller continued, "and she discovered the rafter and Shen I's magic pill. She paused for just a moment, turning it over in her hand. Then she ate it. A moment later, she found herself floating—floating softly and steadily into the sky and up to the Moon.

Everyone looked up at the Moon, the children and the adults alike. They watched in silence and waited to see the goddess.

"The Moon was bright and brilliant that night, just like it is tonight," the storyteller told the children. "Like a crystal ball as clear as glass and as bright and beautiful as shining water. Heng 'O landed on the Moon and found herself alone in a forest of cinnamon trees. She sat beneath the trees and vomited the pill she swallowed just moments before. To her amazement, a white rabbit appeared in front of her, and he welcomed her to the Moon."

The children sat enrapt, listening to the story. They knew the storyteller told the truth, because now, as they looked up, they could see Heng 'O dancing, and they could see the rabbit silhouetted against the Moon.

"If Shen I were to see his wife, he too would have to fly to the sky," the storyteller explained. "And Emperor Yao gave the Divine Archer the Palace of the Sun and a golden bird to take him there. He also gave him a mooncake to protect him from the solar heat and a lunar talisman that would enable him to travel across the sky to visit Heng 'O in the Moon."

The children listened intently. They knew about mooncakes and they knew about magic. They knew that mooncakes brought good luck and happiness, for their mothers had told them so. They had eaten the mooncakes and felt the magic for themselves.

"But the lunar talisman," the storyteller continued, "held even more magic than mooncakes. And when Shen I wore this talisman around his neck, he drifted from this golden Sun palace to the Moon, and there he united with his lovely wife." Shen I loved his wife, and he chopped down the cinnamon trees on the

Moon and built her a lovely palace. Heng 'O lived in her palace with her white rabbit, and Shen I lived in his palace with his golden bird. But life was hard for Shen I and Heng 'O after that. Banished to the Moon, Heng 'O could never visit the Sun palace, and though the talisman held powerful magic, it would only allow her husband to travel to her once a month. He then had to return to his part of the sky—and leave his wife in darkness.

"Heng 'O pined for her husband," the storyteller told them. "She pined away each time he left, growing dimmer and dimmer the farther he got from her lunar palace. The goddess was sad. Each month, by the time Shen I returned to his Sun palace, Heng 'O had faded from sight, and disappeared."

The children's faces saddened as the storyteller told this part of the tale, for they hated to think of the goddess alone in the darkness.

"But when Shen I came to her, Heng 'O was happy," the storyteller reassured them. And the children smiled.

"She waited in darkness until he left his solar palace, but she got brighter and brighter the closer he came. By the time he arrived, she shone brightly and brilliantly, just like she is now.

"He is there with her now," the storyteller said, widening his eyes and nodding his head. "On the fifteenth of each month, Shen I rides to the Moon on a sunbeam to visit Heng 'O. He gets closer and closer, and she shines brighter and brighter. Then she becomes the radiant goddess that dances above us now, shining with love and happiness and a bit of moon magic."

* *

"Heng 'O and her Palace on the Moon" was adapted from stories of Heng 'O that appear in E. C. Krupp's *Beyond the Blue Horizon: Myths and Legends of the Sun, Moon, Stars, and Planets* (New York: Oxford University Press, 1991), in Edward T. C. Werner's *Ancient Tales and Folklore of China* (London: George Harap, 1995), and on various Internet sites.

THE SCIENCE OF THE MOON

BELIEF: There are inhabitants on the Moon.

Since ancient times when people believed that powerful gods inhabited the sky, Moon gazers saw images in the patterns of light and dark on the lunar surface. Quite often they saw a goddess, like Heng 'O, and quite often they told myths of her lunar palace and of how she arrived on the Moon. To some people the moon spots looked like toads and to others they looked like hares or rabbits. To some people the patterns looked like the groves of trees, to others a girl and a boy, and to others the man in the Moon people often speak of today.

Since the time when early people explained moon spots as lunar inhabitants, scientists have studied the topography of the Moon and identified the lunar features as highlands and craters. The craters are the dark spots; the largest ones are called *oceans* and the smaller ones are called *seas*. People always connected the Moon with water, in part because of its influence on the tides. Then, when the sixteenth-century astronomer Galileo looked through his telescope at the surface of the Moon, he thought the dark spots looked like water. So he named them *maria*, after the Latin word for sea.

The Moon's maria, or craters, formed billions of years ago in the beginning stages of the universe, when meteoroids slammed into the Moon and molten lava flowed up to the surface. Some scientists long ago thought the dark spots on the Moon were volcanoes, and much later scientists did discover volcanoes on the Moon. But these volcanoes erupted in the beginning stages of the universe and have been extinct for a long time. Though the craters of the Moon are nothing but volcanic rock, the name Galileo gave them stuck. Numerous "seas" comprise the nearside of the Moon and many more comprise the far side. The light areas of the Moon are called *highlands* and they're composed of a rock called *anorthosite*.

The Moon may not have water on its surface but it does influence the water on Earth. The Moon's phases and its gravity cause the ocean tides. When the Moon is facing the Earth, the gravitational force of the Moon pulls at the oceans on that part of the Earth's surface and causes a bulge in the water we call high tide or spring tide. When the oceans on one side of the Earth experience high tide, the oceans on the other side of the Earth experience low tide, or neap tide. That's because the gravitational force of the Moon is weaker the farther the Moon gets from the Earth. Because the Earth rotates on its axis every 24 hours, on any given place on Earth two high tides and two low tides occur in 24 hours.

BELIEF: The Moon is able to be colonized.

Heng 'O lived quite comfortably on the Moon in her palace made of cinnamon trees, but no trees of any kind could possibly grow on the Moon. No one could live there either—not yet anyway. For one thing, there's no water, at least no water that scientists know how to tap. But there has been a lot of discussion about colonizing the Moon, and scientists continually debate the possibilities for tapping into the Moon's natural resources and perhaps giving the Moon some of the Earth's resources in return.

For people to live on the Moon they would have to depend on the Earth's resources because the Moon has neither water nor air. It has no nitrogen either, so plants cannot grow there. Also, the temperature varies drastically depending on the Moon's proximity to the Sun. This makes the Moon either much too hot or much too cold to support life of any kind. For people to live on the Moon scientists would need to develop techniques for mining the Moon's surface and they would need to figure out how to supply the air and water needed to support life. Improvements would also need to take place in space transportation. Right now it takes several days to get to the Moon by rocket. Traveling back and forth to obtain necessary resources would be much too costly and time-consuming.

Most scientists agree that the Earth is the only planet that currently supports life, and many believe that Mars is a much more likely site than the Moon for future colonization. Apollo astronauts who landed on the Moon brought back samples of the Moon's soil, and an analysis of those samples revealed that the Moon differs from the Earth significantly in its composition and resources.

BELIEF: The Moon has a relationship with the Sun,
and the Sun makes the Moon shine.

The marriage of the Moon goddess and the Sun god appeared in the myths of many cultures, and this marriage reflected a knowledge of the Moon's relationship to the Sun. The story of the marriage between Shen I and Heng 'O illustrates the interdependence of the Sun and the Moon and the concept of *yin* and *yang*, the idea that everything in the universe has an opposite and that a balance between the two opposites keeps the universe moving in recurrent cycles.

The marriage of the Sun and Moon represents the union of yin and yang, but it also explains the Moon's changing phases. In the myth of Heng 'O, the Sun god illuminated the Moon. She got fuller and more brilliant as her husband headed toward her each month to visit her in her lunar palace.

The Sun does illuminate the Moon; but how the Sun illuminates it depends on the relative positions of the Sun, Moon, and Earth. Though the myth of Heng 'O reflects an awareness that the positions of the Sun and the Moon cause the Moon's phases, it shows no awareness that the Earth has anything to do with it. As Shen I comes close to his wife, she grows fuller and fuller, and as Shen I moves away from his wife, she pines away and disappears. The full moon actually occurs when the Sun and Moon are far apart, however, and a new moon actually occurs when they're close together. In fact, the Moon grows larger the farther it gets from the Sun, and the Moon grows smaller the closer it gets. Figure 2.1 shows the lunar phases as they appear from Earth.

In "Heng 'O and Her Palace on the Moon," the Sun god moves toward the Moon goddess. In the chapter on the Sun we learned that the Sun's movement is just an illusion and that the Earth is actually moving around the Sun. Because the relative positions of the Sun, Moon, and Earth determine how much of the Moon is illuminated, we know now that the Moon, and not the Sun, moves through the sky. We know also that the Moon doesn't grow and shrink, but that it appears to grow and shrink because the portion we see illuminated changes as the Moon revolves around the Earth.

FIGURE 2.1 · The Lunar Phases

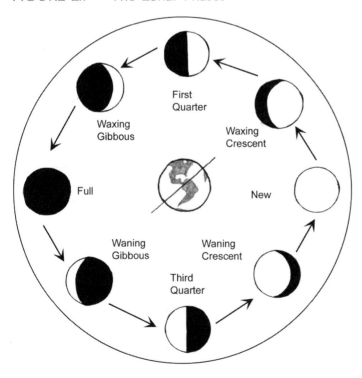

BELIEF: The Moon moves through a continuous cycle.

While the story of Heng 'O and Shen I explains the union of yin and yang and the changing phases of the Moon it also explains the concept of lunar renewal. When the Moon waxes and wanes, symbolically it dies and then returns to life. That's what makes mythological Moon goddesses immortal. The Moon continually renews itself, and the cycle of lunar phases confirms the goddesses' ability to live forever.

Figure 2.1 shows how the phases of the Moon look from Earth. If you were on the Moon you would see the Earth go through these same phases. When the Moon is less than half illuminated, it is said to be in its *crescent phase*. When the Moon is more than half illuminated, it is said to be in its *gibbous phase*. A waning Moon appears to be getting smaller, and a waxing Moon appears to be getting larger. Because the Moon revolves around the Earth, and because it revolves completely around the Earth in one month, the Moon goes through all its phases during that time. Then it begins again.

Anyone who observes the Moon over a month's time knows that the Moon waxes and wanes and that it returns to a full, round ball every month. Because the Moon could die and return to life and because it followed a continual cycle, people learned to keep time by counting the days from full Moon to full Moon. Usually, one full Moon occurs each month, so early people called one month one "Moon." A "blue Moon" refers to a full Moon that appears for the second time in any calendar month. This usually only happens about once every two and a half years, which explains why the expression "once in a blue Moon" means only once in a long while.

BELIEF: The Moon has seasonal significance.

Moon goddesses had magic powers; when they waxed and waned they appeared to die and resurrect, and as they continued this cycle they appeared to turn the seasons. Ancient people did not know that the seasons changed because the Earth moved around the Sun; they simply structured their lives by the rhythms of nature. Ancient farmers assigned each season significance by connecting it with agricultural rituals, and ancient hunters assigned each season significance by connecting it with the migration of game animals. The Moon changed and it set a pattern. Farmers used that pattern to learn when to plant and when to harvest, and hunters used that pattern to learn when to return to the hunting grounds.

From ancient times, people learned to construct calendars based on the cycle of the Moon. Each year contained twelve months, but because early calendar makers kept time from full Moon to full Moon, twelve Moon months did not add up to a 365-day year. We know that one year is 365 days because that's how long it takes the Earth to revolve around the Sun, and twelve Moon months is eleven days shorter than that. So calendars based on the movement of the Sun eventually replaced these lunar calendars. Solar calendars still had to make up for the fact that it actually takes the Earth a few hours longer than 365 days to revolve around the Sun. That's why we have leap year—to make up the difference.

BELIEF: The Moon brings good luck and happiness.

The belief in the Moon's ability to bring good luck and happiness stems from its connection to the seasons, and particularly to the harvest. The harvest Moon is a full Moon that occurs each year nearest to the autumn equinox, which in ancient times occurred in mid-August. The Moon appears on the horizon just as the Sun sets at this time of year, and it shines there brightly for several days in a row. Because the harvest Moon is closer to the horizon it seems bigger and brighter than any other moon, even though it's really the same size. In agricultural communities, farmers used the extra hours of light to harvest their crops. They also considered the harvest Moon a blessing from the gods for a fruitful season.

For centuries people from all over the world held harvest Moon festivals, and in China even today people continue to celebrate the harvest Moon. The Chinese hold a festival, which they call Yue Ping, and they honor Heng 'O, their Moon goddess, by baking round mooncakes and exchanging the cakes with their friends and family and rewarding their goddess for her influence over the year's crops. Heng 'O is a particularly celebrated Moon goddess, but Moon goddesses from other cultures were traditionally female. These female Moon goddesses were believed to control the cycles of seasons and the fertility of the Earth.

— TOPICS FOR DISCUSSION AND PROJECTS

TOPIC 1. Lunar Spots

Myths from all over the world give explanations for Moon spots, and those explanations form the base for captivating tales of goddesses and animals who live in the Moon. "The Man in the Moon" Web site, listed below, shows different images people saw in the pattern of dark and light on the lunar surface. Some of the books in the Suggested Reading list contain Moon legends that explain why those images appear, and they offer speculations on just who might live in the magical Moon land they imagined.

PROJECT IDEA

View the Web sites listed below to see pictures of the images people have identified in the pattern of Moon spots. Then have students draw their own images of what they see when they look at the Moon. Perhaps they see a rabbit, or a toad, or two children, or a man, or perhaps they see something different. Have them write a story about the character they see. They might want to include elements that appear in other lunar myths that indicate ancient perceptions of the lunar sphere. The following list represents some lunar traits that might give students ideas for their stories.

1. Immortality

2. Connection with water

3. Connection to harvest, good fortune

4. Ability to heal and revive

SUGGESTED READING

Light, Michael. *Full Moon*. New York: Knopf, 1999.

> Contains 129 photographs of the Moon from Apollo missions, including some that show intricate detail of the Moon's craters. Captions and explanations accompany the photos.

Long, Hua. *The Moon Maiden and Other Asian Folktales*. San Francisco: China Books and Periodicals, Inc.: 1993.

Moroney, Lynn. *Moontellers: Myths of the Moon from Around the World.* Flagstaff, AZ: Northland Publishing, 1995.

> Contains myths and legends of the Moon from many different cultures, including China, and contains lots of illustrations of lunar images from folklore.

O'Hara, Gwydion. *Moon Lore: Myths and Folklore from Around the World.* St. Paul, MN: Llewellyn, 1997.

Sanders, Ian. "Images Seen in the Maria of the Moon." *http://www.planetfusion.co.uk/~pignut/images.html.*

Sanders, Ian. "The Man in the Moon." *http://www.planetfusion.co.uk/~pignut/man_in_moon.html.*

> Contains legends from around the world, including China. Click on "How to See the Man in the Moon" to get images commonly recognized on the lunar surface.

Because the full Moon represented the goddess in her renewed form and because it provided light to both hunters and farmers, the full Moon enjoyed a special place in myth and in calendar making. People in many cultures gave names to each full Moon, and these names typically reflected its significance to a certain time of year.

PROJECT IDEA

Have students choose one of the following names for the full Moon and write a myth that explains its seasonal significance. Short descriptions help explain each full Moon listed below. The sources in the Suggested Reading section give further details about these Moons and myths that might stimulate story ideas.

January—Wolf Moon, Winter Moon

February—Snow Moon, Hunger Moon, Trapper's Moon

March—Worm Moon, Sap Moon, Maple Sugar Moon, Big Clouds Moon

April—Pink Moon, Grass Moon, Planter's Moon, Seed Moon, Frog's Croak Moon

May—Flower Moon, Budding Moon, Hare Moon, Corn Planting Moon

June—Strawberry Moon, Honey Moon, Salmon Fishing Moon

July—Buck Moon, Killer Whale Moon, Thunder Moon

August—Sturgeon Moon, Grain Moon, Collecting Food Moon

September—Harvest Moon, Fruit Moon, Leaf Fall Moon

October—Hunter's Moon, Blood Moon, Falling River Moon

November—Beaver Moon, Frosty Moon, Every Buck Loses Its Horns Moon

December—Oak Moon, Cold Moon, Big Freezing Moon

SUGGESTED READING

Farmers' Almanac. "Full Moon Names and Their Meanings." *http://www.farmers almanac.com/astronomy/fullmoonnames.html.*

Explains the significance and origin assigned to the names of the full moons.

McCurdy, Michael. *An Algonquin Year: The Year According to the Full Moon.* Boston: Houghton Mifflin, 2000.

Chronicles the full Moons by month and connects them to seasonal activities of the Algonquin, which explain the full Moon's names.

TOPIC 3. The Moon Illusion

The Moon illusion is an optical illusion that makes the Moon look larger when it's near the horizon. Some scientists say that this occurs because the thicker air near the horizon makes the Moon appear bigger and brighter than when it's higher in the sky. Others say that the illusion occurs because we're fooled into comparing the big, bright moon with other objects we see on the horizon, and the Moon overpowers them. The Sun does the same thing, though it's dangerous to look directly at the Sun.

The Moon illusion has puzzled people for years, and astronomers, philosophers, psychologists, and other scholars have attempted to explain this phenomenon. Numerous other illusions appear in nature and in the atmosphere as well, and they all contribute to our perception of the sky as a place of wonder and magic.

PROJECT IDEA

Use the suggested readings below to teach students about other astronomical illusions that have perplexed people over the years. Optical illusions of any kind have always fascinated people. It's amazing to see how the mind processes such deceptive images. Have an optical illusion lab in your classroom. Students can choose illusions they read about in the sources below or in other books on optical illusions and present them as an activity in your lab. Have students explain how different optical illusions work.

SUGGESTED READING

DiSpezio, Michael Anthony. *Eye-Popping Optical Illusions*. New York: Sterling, 2001.

> Contains numerous projects on visual illusions for use in the classroom.

Gallant, Roy A. *Rainbows, Mirages, and Sundogs: The Sky as a Source of Wonder*. New York: Atheneum, 1997.

> Aimed at children ages 9–12. Explains numerous special effects in the sky and atmosphere. Includes diagrams and experiments.

Joyce, Katherine. *Astounding Optical Illusions*. New York: Sterling, 1995.

> Contains examples of optical designs and explanations of how the mind processes them. Explains scientific phenomena such as the mirage and other illusions.

"Optical Illusion Websites." *http://www.sandlotscience.com*.

> Contains links to numerous optical illusion sites on the Web, including those on the Moon illusion.

Simon, Seymour. *Now You See It, Now You Don't*. New York: William Morrow, 1998.

> Classic book on optical illusions involving distance, depth, brightness, and color. Contains numerous illusions and their explanations.

Unruh, J. Timothy. *Impossible Optical Illusions to Confound and Astound*. New York: Sterling, 2002.

> Contains numerous illusions and explains how they fool the mind and eye.

TOPIC 4. The Principle of Yin and Yang

In the myth of Heng 'O, both the Moon goddess and the rabbit represented the female force, the essence of yin, which then combined with the male force, yang. Myths often expressed conflicts between opposing forces—between gods of light and gods of darkness, and between gods of the Sun and gods of the rain. Mythmakers recognized opposites in the world, but they also knew that these opposites depended on each other. Too much of one thing meant death to the world. Too much rain caused flood, so the world needed something to counteract the rain. Too much Sun caused drought, and ten Suns in the sky could reduce the world to ashes.

The concept of yin and yang is essential to Chinese thought, which involves both the belief in original chaos and the subsequent separation of chaos into yin and yang. Yin and yang are generally considered abstract forces, but mythologists turned the abstract into concepts they could understand. Mythologists recognized the existence of opposites, so they assigned names to the opposing forces—male and female, light and dark, rain and drought, Sun god and Moon goddess. In the myth, Heng 'O represented the cold, watery female principle, and Shen I represented the warm, male principle. In Chinese belief, it is through this balance of the two that all things exist.

PROJECT IDEA

Show students the Chinese symbol of yin and yang. This symbol shows how opposites come together to form a full circle. Let students use the lists below to learn what characteristics the Chinese associated with yin and yang forces. Then have students design their own symbols that represent a union of opposites, or a union of Sun and Moon.

Yang forces	Yin forces
Heat	Cold
Drought	Water
Sun	Moon
Sky	Earth
Male	Female
Square	Round

SUGGESTED READING

Appelbaum, Stanley. *Traditional Chinese Designs*. Mineola, NY: Dover, 1989.

Bruce-Mitford, Miranda. *Illustrated Book of Signs and Symbols*. Mineola, NY: Dover, 1996.

> Standard reference work available in many libraries. Contains color illustrations of signs and symbols in nature and in other subject areas. Includes symbols of the Sun and Moon.

"Chinese Clip Arts." *http://www.in4mation.org*.

One of the numerous Web sites of Chinese clip art. Contains patterns, calligraphy, and many other kinds of designs from Chinese culture.

Williams, Charles Alfred Speed. *Chinese Symbolism and Art Motifs*. Revised ed. Boston: Charles E. Tuttle, 1989.

Contains 400 illustrations of the yin yang symbol and others, and explains their historical and cultural significance.

TOPIC 5. Colonizing the Moon

Scientists continue to debate whether it is feasible to colonize the Moon. Some argue that it is the best place in the solar system for future development, while others argue that Mars is the best place.

PROJECT IDEA

Read students the arguments some scientists give for developing a colony on the Moon, and read them the arguments other scientists give for developing a colony on Mars. Then divide your class into two groups. Have one group plan a colony on the Moon and the other group plan a colony on Mars. Have them explain what supplies they would need and where they would get them.

SUGGESTED READING

Benford, Gregory, and George Zebraski, eds. *Skylife: Space Habitats in Story and Science*. New York: Harcourt, 2000.

> Contains science fact and fiction in a collection of stories and essays by well-known science fiction authors such as Isaac Asimov and Ray Bradbury. Has color illustrations and much information on space colonization.

Cole, Michael D. *Moon Base: First Colony in Space*. Berkeley Heights, NJ: Enslow, 1999.

> Concentrates largely on Galileo's unmanned space mission and contains lots of color illustrations and artists' depictions of a Moon base.

Dyson, Marianne. *Home on the Moon: Living on a Space Frontier*. Washington, DC: National Geographic Press, 2003.

> Includes lots of information about Moon colonization. Has images and activities and descriptions and artists' depictions of what a Moon colony would look like.

Lewis, John S. *Mining the Sky*. New York: Perseus Publishing, 1997.

> Geared more toward teachers than students, but explores the possibility of exploiting mineral resources from the Moon and planets.

TOPIC 6. The Chinese Moon Festival

Each year on September 20 or 21 in China, the Moon is at its maximum brightness. This is when the people celebrate the Moon Festival, also called the Mid-Autumn Harvest Festival. During this festival, Chinese children learn the story of the goddess Heng 'O, who took a pill of immortality and ascended to the Moon, where she has lived ever since. Some say that every year on September 20 or 21, Heng 'O is most beautiful, and others say that this is the time when Heng 'O dances on the Moon. The people see her when they gaze up at the lunar surface. Her story is famous throughout China, and so is her festival.

PROJECT IDEA

Hold a Harvest Moon Festival in your classroom. Divide the class into groups. Have some of the children read aloud to the class some of Moon myths listed in the section below. Have some other children make mooncakes to serve to the class during your festival. Have others decorate the classroom with lunar symbols, and have others create posters to hang in the classroom that relate lunar facts and superstitions.

SUGGESTED READING

Markham, Lois. *Harvest*. Woodbridge, CT: Blackbirch, 1998.

> Includes informative facts and customs associated with harvest festivals from many cultures, including the Chinese Mid-Autumn Harvest Festival. Touches on the celebration of life and the cycles of life and of the harvest and the seasons. Includes festivals and celebrations from Brazil, England, India, Israel, Japan, China, Mexico, Nigeria, Puerto Rico, Russia, and the United States.

Simonds, Nina, and Leslie Swartz. *Moonbeams, Dumplings, and Dragon Boats: A Treasury of Chinese Holiday Tales, Activities and Recipes*. New York: Harcourt, 2002.

> Contains myths and stories of the festivals, including the Moon Festival. Has ideas for celebrating, including suggestions for activities and recipes for mooncakes.

Stepanchuk, Carol. *Mooncakes and Hungry Ghosts: Festivals in China*. San Francisco: China Books and Periodicals, Inc., 1992.

> Discusses Chinese festivals, customs, and traditions. Includes a detailed description of the Moon Festival.

Stepanchuk, Carol. *Red Eggs and Dragon Boats: Celebrating Chinese Festivals*. Berkeley, CA: Pacific View Press, 1994.

Covers five Chinese festivals and discusses the customs and traditions connected with each. Includes information on the Moon Festival and recipes for mooncakes.

Tan, Amy. *The Moon Lady*. New York: Atheneum, 1992

Adapted from Amy Tan's adult novel *The Joy Luck Club*. Recounts the events of the Chinese Moon Festival through the eyes of a young girl.

—— SUGGESTED READING FOR TEACHERS

Brueton, Diana. *Many Moons*. New York: Prentice Hall, 1991.

> Contains legends, lore, and superstitions of the Moon as well as some science. Has lots of beautiful illustrations.

Harley, Timothy. *Moon Lore*. Carlisle, MA: Charles River Books, 1976.

> A reprint of Timothy Harley's classic book on Moon legends from around the world. Reprint and original available in many libraries.

Krupp, E. C. "Midautumn Moon Goddess." *Sky and Telescope* 86, 3 (1993): 59–60.

Moroney, Lynn. *Moontellers: Myths of the Moon from Around the World*. Flagstaff, AZ: Northland Publishing, 1995.

> Contains myths and legends of the Moon from many different cultures, including China. Has lots of illustrations of lunar images from folklore.

NASA and Montana State University. "CERES (Center for Educational Resources) Project." *http://btc.montana.edu/ceres*.

> Contains interactive K–12 science activities using NASA resources. Activities include those on Moon myths and legends and birthday moons, as well as many on other areas of astronomy.

Ross, Helen, and Cornelius Plug. *The Moon Illusion*. New York: Oxford University Press, 2002.

> Discusses various explanations for the Moon illusion that have surfaced over the centuries in philosophy, psychology, science, and mathematics.

Werner, Edward T. C. *Ancient Tales and Folklore of China*. London: George Harap, 1995.

3 · The Stars and Constellations

THE MYTHS OF THE STARS AND CONSTELLATIONS

The stars of the night sky have captivated skywatchers all over the world with their beauty. In times long ago when no artificial lights polluted the heavens, the mysterious night lights appeared out of the darkness like magic and looked down on the Earth like thousands of sparkling eyes. In some ancient myths the stars represented fires that lit the pathway to heaven, and in others they represented glittering jewels in the palaces of sky gods. People everywhere searched for an explanation for the stars that lit their world, and mythmakers attempted to make sense of their arrangement by assigning pictures to the patterns those celestial lights appeared to form in the heavens.

Constellations arose as figments of the imagination. It is difficult to see the objects and animals people assigned to certain star groups, but assigning pictures to the stars helped people organize the sky. Early people named constellations all over the night sky, but the twelve most familiar constellations constitute the zodiac. The first zodiac probably arose in ancient Babylon, but the most familiar zodiac today arose in Greece. Aries is considered the leader of the zodiac. Aries is a faint constellation, but its position in the sky made it prominent in myths and legends. About 2,000 years ago, the Sun passed through Aries on the first day of spring, so people used this star group as a seasonal marker. To many people spring marked the beginning of the year, a time when the Earth renewed itself after a winter death. When the Sun passed through Aries the year began.

Read the following myth of Aries that surfaced in the Greek story of the ram with the golden fleece. This story explains how the ram rose to the sky to live among the stars. Then read The Science of the Stars and Constellations section to learn some facts about the stars and use the topics for discussion and projects to stimulate ideas for student research.

"THE RAM WITH THE GOLDEN FLEECE," A MYTH FROM GREECE

Far above the Earth, on a mountain in the clouds, lived the most powerful gods of ancient Greece. These gods ruled the Earth, sea, and sky from their sacred dwelling place far out of reach of mortal beings. The name of this sacred place was Mount Olympus, and Zeus served as king in this mountain paradise. His power extended throughout the sky, and he commanded the gods and goddesses who ruled the clouds and the rain and all the other forces of nature. Often he sent thunderous booms and lightning strikes through the sky to show the strength of his power.

Mount Olympus rose to the heavens and it sheltered the gods from the powerful forces that ravaged the Earth. A thick wall of billowing clouds surrounded the sacred mountain, so no one could see the gods who lived there. Everyone in Greece knew that the gods did live there, however. They knew that all sorts of immortal beings lived in the sky. Sometimes, the people could see animals that the gods placed in the sky world with them, glittering like shining stars in the dark night. Sometimes the people saw a bull shining brightly in the dark night, and the people were told that Zeus placed him among the stars to thank the bull for helping him secure the affections of Europa, the mortal daughter of King Agenor. Sometimes they saw a crab shining brightly in the night, and they were told that Zeus's wife Hera placed the bull among the stars to reward him for attacking Hercules, one of Hera's mortal enemies.

The people of Greece saw many animals living among the stars, and over time they heard a story that explained how each of those animals got there. They couldn't see all of the animals at the same time, but they saw all of them over the course of a year. They learned that people long before them had seen these animals too.

The children of ancient Greece were delighted that animals lived in the sky, and they were delighted that the gods had placed them there to reward their good deeds. Sometimes the stories saddened the children because the animals had to die on Earth before they rose to the stars. The stories also comforted the children, however, because they knew that the gods had rescued the animals from death and allowed them to live in the sky forever.

One story that particularly delighted the children was the story of the ram. This story involved a king and a cloud fairy, and it told how the ram came to the aid of two children who suffered at the hands of their cruel stepmother. Nephele, the cloud fairy, lived on Mount Olympus, but she descended to Earth and fell in love with King Athamas. Nephele and the king had two children together, Phrixus and Helle. Now Greek mythology is full of tales of gods and goddesses who traveled back and forth from Mount Olympus, and who fell in love and married mortals. But unless the gods chose to place the mortals in the sky world as they did the animals, the mortals had to remain on Earth. Sooner or later, the gods and goddesses who loved them had to return to the sky.

When Nephele returned to the sky, she left Phrixus and Helle on Earth with their father. The king soon married again, this time to a cruel woman named Ino. Ino also had two children with the king, and once her own children were born, she decided to do everything she could to ensure that her son and not Phrixus, the king's first-born, inherited the throne. Crazy with jealousy over her husband's first children, Ino plotted with the other women of the village to burn the fields and cause a great famine that would threaten the land.

"I must destroy the grain to secure my children's future," she told the women of the village. The women believed her. When the parched fields produced nothing more of substance, the people began to suffer and many of them died.

Now it seems curious that Ino thought a plan such as this would secure her children's future. But people in those times believed that sacrifices to the gods relieved famines and plagues to the land, and Ino tricked her husband into believing Zeus had demanded that Athamas sacrifice his children, Phrixus and Helle, to restore the land to fruitfulness. Athamas loved his children, but he was a dedicated king, and his evil wife convinced him that nothing short of sacrificing the children would save his people. So Athamas sent Phrixus and Helle to the sacrificial altar. But gods and goddesses who had the power to reward good deeds also had the power to punish bad deeds. The gods and goddesses of Olympus saw what was happening on Earth, and they gathered together to save Nephele's children. Hermes, the messenger god, sent to the altar Khrysomallos, a beautiful magic ram who had wings and fleece made of gold and who could whisk the children away and carry them on his back through the sky. Khrysomallos swooped onto the altar and saved the children just in time. Up and away he sailed into the clouds and across the Black Sea. Helle lost her grip and fell, but Poseidon, the sea god, rescued her and turned her into a sea nymph. Phrixus held tight to the ram's neck the rest of the way, and in a short while he arrived safely in Colchus.

When Khrysomallos landed with Phrixus on his back, King Aeëtes received the young prince and welcomed him into his kingdom. The ram begged Phrixus to sacrifice him to the gods and to remove his golden fleece and present it as a gift to his new king. Phrixus did as he was asked. Aeëtes accepted the gift and hung the golden fleece in a garden. There, it bathed the sky with a golden glow. Phrixus married the king's daughter Chalciope and assumed his rightful place as royalty. Zeus descended from Mount Olympus and carried Khrysomallos to the sky where he could live forever. And the ram took his rightful place among the stars.

. . . .

"The Ram with the Golden Fleece" was adapted from accounts of the original legend reproduced in *A Handbook of Greek Mythology*, by H. J. Rose (New York: Dutton, 1959), and from accounts of the myth on numerous astronomy and mythology sites on the Internet.

THE SCIENCE OF THE STARS AND CONSTELLATIONS

The myth of the ram with the golden fleece is just one of many star myths; there's a myth for each one of the constellations of the zodiac and for many other constellations as well. There are also myths for many, many of the individual stars. The myth of the ram has significance because Aries the ram is the first constellation of the zodiac and it serves as the leader. "The Ram with the Golden Fleece" explains how Aries ascended to the sky, but it also explains why the stars in the constellation are so dim—because the ram no longer has its golden fleece.

BELIEF: The stars and constellations appear in the heavens for a reason.

Myths that explain the origin of the constellations tell how those groups of stars got into the sky. Usually the constellations represent people or animals that the myths say existed on Earth and were immortalized in the heavens. Often, they arose to the sky world through the workings of some powerful god.

In reality, stars formed in the heavens. They formed from collapsing clouds of gas and dust. These clouds are called *nebulae* and the gas inside them is primarily hydrogen. When these clouds collapse the pressure inside them builds, and nuclear fusion ignites the hydrogen. Then a star is born. That star is simply a burning ball of hydrogen gas, and it shines until it uses up all the hydrogen it has.

BELIEF: The stars form patterns in the sky.

Constellations are figments of the imagination. For thousands of years people connected the dots of celestial light to create pictures to help them identify the stars and remember their arrangement in the heavens. There are about 400 billion stars in the Milky Way galaxy alone, and it's difficult to distinguish one from the other. People created constellations to help. They used the pictures they "drew" in the heavens to identify an ordered arrangement and to help them name and remember the locations of individual stars.

Astronomers today divide the sky into eighty-eight constellations, and those eighty-eight constellations contain all the stars we can see. Long ago this was not the case. The Navajo people of the American Southwest told a myth to explain why stars appeared outside the constellations they recognized. Black God was the primary Navajo deity, and he planned to create one constellation to represent each animal on earth. So he placed crystals in the sky in patterns, and he placed them in an ordered arrangement from east to west. Coyote was the trickster god of Navajo myths, and he was always creating trouble. Coyote stole Black God's crystals and threw some of them randomly into the heavens. That's why, the Navajo say, there are many stars in the night sky that fit into no pattern at all.

BELIEF: The zodiacal constellations form a circle
around the sky.

The name zodiac means "circle of animals," and this circle refers to the ecliptic, an imaginary path that marks the apparent movement of the Sun across the sky. Look at Figure 3.1, which shows the path of the ecliptic.

FIGURE 3.1 · The Path of the Ecliptic

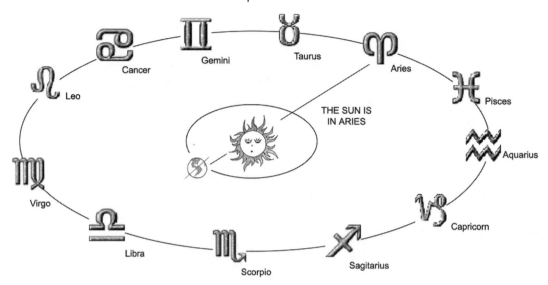

Though we know that the Sun only appears to move because the Earth orbits around it, the Sun appears to travel along the ecliptic, and along the way the traveling Sun passes twelve groups of stars that constitute all the signs of the zodiac. All but two of these zodiac signs are animals—Virgo the virgin and Libra the scales. The Sun makes one complete circle around the ecliptic each year, passing in front of one constellation of the zodiac each month. When you hear someone say, for example, "The Sun is in Cancer," that means that the Sun is passing in front of the constellation the ancient Greeks named Cancer the crab. People born at that time of year have Cancer the crab as their zodiac sign. This sign is also called their Sun sign. Their Moon sign represents the zodiacal constellations where the Moon appeared at the time of their birth.

BELIEF: Different stars and constellations appear in the sky throughout the year.

To people who didn't know that the Earth revolved around the Sun, the Sun appeared to move against the background of fixed stars. Astronomers use the term "fixed stars" to distinguish the stars from the planets. Planets wander back and forth across the sky because like the Earth, they constantly orbit the Sun. Stars are in constant motion too;

it's just difficult for us to detect the movement because it happens over the course of a year. The entire sky appears to rotate as the Earth revolves around the Sun, and skywatchers know that as they watch the heavens, the constellations that dominate the sky change. Skywatchers long ago began to notice when the constellations first appeared and when they disappeared. The stars rose and set, but they always remained in the same formations. During the course of a year, skywatchers at one given place on Earth saw different constellations rise and set at different times.

Several thousand years ago when Aries rose into the sky on the first day of spring, the ram earned his role as leader of the zodiac. Today Aries still serves as leader but it no longer marks the first day of spring; Pisces does. This is due to precession of the *equinoxes*, the slow westward movement of the Sun across the background of stars. The Sun appeared against the stars of Aries at the vernal equinox, but over the centuries the Sun moved westward against the background of stars. At the vernal equinox today, it appears against the stars of Pisces. Pisces is one constellation west of Aries in the sky. It takes 26,000 years for the Sun to move completely around the ecliptic and pass in front of each constellation of the zodiac; so in the course of 26,000 years each sign of the zodiac takes its turn as leader. The gravity of the Moon and the Sun pulls on the Earth at the equator and makes the planet wobble, and this causes the constellations to appear in the sky over the Earth over a long period of time. Aries won't truly serve as leader of the zodiac again for about 23,000 years.

BELIEF: The appearance of stars in the sky signals
seasonal changes on Earth.

Taurus

You often hear people explain that the seasons change because the
Sun is farther from the Earth at some times than at others. This isn't
so, however. The Sun is always the same distance from the Earth. The
seasons change because the Earth's axis tilts, and to observers on Earth,
this tilt makes the Sun appear higher in the sky at some times of year
than at others. When the Sun is highest above Earth, it takes longer to
set and we have more hours of daylight. But because the Earth rotates
on its axis and revolves around the Sun, when people on one side of
the Earth have more hours of daylight, people on the other side have
fewer hours. When it's summer in the Northern Hemisphere, it's winter
in the Southern Hemisphere—and the other way around.

Gemini

Because people of ancient times noticed that the Sun moved through all twelve constellations in the course of one year, they associated each constellation of the zodiac with a different season. The seasonal connection of each constellation appeared to have influenced the pictures early people assigned to these star groups. When the Sun moved through a constellation in the summer, they connected it to an image they associated with summer. When the Sun moved through a constellation in the winter, fall, or spring, they connected it to an image they associated with those seasons as well.

Leo

The first yearly appearance of a constellation in the predawn sky is called the *heliacal rise* of that constellation. In ancient times the heliacal rise of Aquarius the water carrier signaled the coming of rain or flood. The heliacal rise of Leo the lion signaled the time of drought, a time when the lions returned from the desert to the river banks to drink. Because Virgo the Virgin carries a sheaf in her hands, the heliacal rise of Virgo signaled the time to harvest the fields.

Scorpio

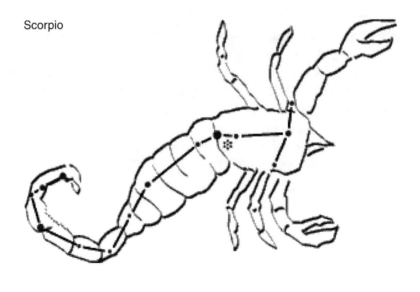

BELIEF: The stars in the sky live forever.

Stars can live for billions of years but they don't live forever; they die. We know that stars are born from collapsing clouds of hydrogen gas. As soon as the hydrogen ignites and begins to burn, the star begins to shine. As soon as the star burns up all of its hydrogen, it dies. A star can die in one of several ways.

Astronomers classify stars by their mass. The mass of a star determines how long it will live and how it will die. Once a star is born and once it begins to shine, it takes its place among the other stars in the sky as a member of the main sequence. Stars spend most of their lives on the main sequence, and most of these stars are less massive than the Sun and rather dim. These dim stars are called *red dwarfs*. They emit a dull red glow, but you can't see them without a telescope. Proxima Centauri is a red dwarf and the closest star to Earth, but we still can't see it without a telescope. Most of the stars we can see are *giants* or *supergiants*. Giants and supergiants are much more massive than the Sun, which means that they'll die much sooner than the Sun. That's because they burn up their hydrogen fuel much faster than stars with less mass. The more massive a star, the faster it burns and the faster it dies; the less massive a star, the slower it burns and the longer it lives.

Many stars begin their lives as dwarfs, turn into giants, and then turn back into dwarfs again toward the end of their lives. In the early stages of stellar evolution, the hydrogen in a young star ignites and releases energy that makes the star get bigger and brighter. It also gets cooler and redder. Then it becomes a *red giant*. Once a star becomes a red giant, a cloud forms around it, and that cloud expands and dissolves into space. The star is then in the final stages of its life. A cloud forms around the dying star and that cloud blows off into space and collapses, leaving only a hot core. With nothing but the hot core left, the star is no longer a giant but a dwarf. We call these stars *white dwarfs* but they can really be red, blue, yellow, or white, depending on how hot they are. White dwarfs are in the last stages of their life, and they die by simply cooling and fading into nothing.

When supergiants die they go through a different process. These very massive stars become *supernovas*; they don't ever become white dwarfs. They don't develop clouds that dissolve in space and they don't simply cool and fade; they explode. These supernovas or exploding stars leave willowy clouds of glowing gas called *nebulae*—and nebulae are some of the most beautiful objects in the universe. Whether giant or supergiant, stars have an amazingly long life span. Our Sun and other stars like it will live for about ten billion years, and even stars that are nearly twice as massive as the Sun will live a few million years. The stars we see tonight sparking in the heavens will continue to light the night sky for a long, long time to come.

— TOPICS FOR DISCUSSION AND PROJECTS

TOPIC 1. Your Zodiac Sign

Over the centuries people have assigned all sorts of significance to the twelve constellations that form a ring around the heavens. People have always tried to find connections between the sky and the Earth, and people have always tried to discover ways that the Sun, Moon, and stars affect people's lives. People who attempt to find these connections today are called astrologers, and unlike astronomers, astrologers don't test their theories through scientific method. In the ancient world, astrology and astronomy were considered one in the same, but today astrology is considered a pseudo-science. Astronomy is real science based on the laws of physics and mathematics.

Astrologers today connect each person's birth date with a certain sign of the zodiac, and they assign specific personality traits to people born at the times of year when those zodiacal constellations dominate the sky. Astrologers today use the signs of the zodiac to create horoscopes, but the creation of horoscopes began long ago and appeared in early almanacs of ancient civilizations.

PROJECT IDEA

Look at the Greek zodiac signs in Table 3.1. Have students identify their zodiac sign and make a book that explains both the myth and the science behind the constellation it represents. They might use either the picture or the symbol of their sign for a cover design. Tell students to recount the Greek myth of their zodiac signs and illustrate their books with images from the myth to embellish the story. Then explain to students the science of their sign. They can draw a small sky map that shows all the stars that make the pattern and they can connect the dots. Have them identify the bright stars in the constellation and tell what time of year it appears in the sky. Then have them explain any other celestial phenomena that might have a connection to their sign. For instance, the Leonid meteor shower is associated with the constellation Leo and the Taurid meteor shower is associated with the constellation Taurus. The Ring Nebula lies in the constellation Scorpio. Students can use the sources in the Suggested Reading section to learn more about their zodiac signs and to locate their place in the sky.

TABLE 3.1 · The Greek Zodiac

Name	Date	Symbol	Sign
Aries	March 21–April 19		
Taurus	April 20–May 20		
Gemini	May 21–June 20		
Cancer	June 21–July 22		
Leo	July 23–August 22		
Virgo	August 23–September 21		
Libra	September 22–October 23		
Scorpio	October 24–November 21		
Sagittarius	November 22–December 21		
Capricorn	December 22–January 19		
Aquarius	January 20–February 18		
Pisces	February 19–March 20		

SUGGESTED READING

Byrd & Block Communications Inc. "Earth & Sky Radio Series." *http://www. earthsky.com.*

> The Earth & Sky Radio Series Web site has dot-to-dot pictures of the constellations.

Lloyd-Jones, Hugh. *Myths of the Zodiac*. London: Duckworth, 1978.

Contains myths of the zodiac and a star map to help identify the constellations in the night sky.

Sharmon-Burke, Juliet, and Jackie Morris. *Stories from the Stars: Greek Myths of the Zodiac*. New York: Abbeville, 1998.

Contains Greek myths of the twelve signs of the zodiac.

TOPIC 2. Giants and Supergiants

Stars come in all shapes and sizes. Stars bigger, or more massive, than the Sun are called giants or supergiants. These are the brightest stars in the night sky. People told myths of these bright stars because they seemed important. To ancient mythmakers, stars that shone exceptionally bright must have supernatural power. The ancient Greeks were one group of people who gave many of these stars myths of their own.

PROJECT IDEA

Have students take a look at Table 3.2, which lists the brightest stars in the sky. Then have them choose one of the stars listed in the table and write a report about it. The report should include both the science of the star and the Greek myth associated with it. Have students draw a picture of the constellation in which the star appears.

Aldebaran—A red giant that marks the eye of Taurus the bull. Shines in the fall and winter sky.

TABLE 3.2 · The Brightest Stars in the Sky

Star	Constellation	Type
Sirius	Canis Major	blue-white main sequence
Arcturus	Boötes	white giant
Vega	Lyra	blue-white supergiant
Capella	Auriga	white giant
Rigel	Orion	blue-white supergiant
Procyon	Canis Minor	white subgiant main sequence
Betelgeuse	Orion	yellow-orange supergiant
Altair	Aquila	blue-white main sequence
Aldebaran	Taurus	yellow giant
Spica	Virgo	blue-white giant
Antares	Scorpius	yellow-orange supergiant
Pollux	Gemini	yellow giant
Formalhaut	Pisces Austrinus	blue-white main sequence
Deneb	Cygnus	blue-white supergiant

Antares—A red giant that marks the heard of Scorpio the scorpion. Ancient mythmakers thought of Antares as an evil presence in the heavens.

Arcturus—The brightest star in the constellation Boötes the herdsman. Shines in the spring sky.

Betelgeuse—A red supergiant in the constellation Orion. Orion is the hunter, and Betelgeuse marks the shoulder this celestial giant.

Capella—The brightest star in the constellation Auriga. Shines on a winter night.

Deneb—A supergiant and the brightest star in the constellation Cygnus the swan. Deneb is one of the most distant bright stars in the sky but visible because it's 100,000 times as bright as the Sun.

Rigel—A blue supergiant and the brightest star in the constellation Orion. Like half the stars in the sky, Rigel is actually a double star, which is a group of two or more stars that are held together by gravity.

Sirius—A giant star in the constellation Canis Major, the big dog, and the brightest star in the night sky. Dominates the winter sky and shines right below the belt of Orion.

SUGGESTED READING

Byrd & Block Communications Inc. "Earth & Sky Radio Series." *http://www. earthsky.com.*

Earth & Sky Radio Series Web site has dot-to-dot pictures of the constellations.

Gallant, Roy. *Private Lives of the Stars.* New York: Macmillan, 1986.

Discusses many aspects of stellar astronomy. Written for children and young adults, and contains sections on each of the brightest stars that appears in the list above. Contains maps of the winter and summer sky.

Peat, Chris. "The Constellations." *http://www.heavens-above.com/constellations.asp.*

This site contains maps and mythology for the eighty-eight constellations.

Rey, H. A. *Find the Constellations.* Boston: Houghton Mifflin, 1976.

This edition of Rey's classic book is geared toward children and is still available in many libraries. Contains information about how the stars formed and where they are located in the sky, as well as myths about each constellation. Contains interactive quizzes and star charts.

TOPIC 3. Star Clusters

Stars are born in *clusters*. Because all the stars born from one cluster contain the same material and are formed at the same time, astronomers study the clusters to learn more about stellar evolution. Thousands of open clusters exist in our galaxy and each of them contains hundreds of stars. Globular clusters exist in the outer parts of our galaxy and can contain a million stars. The stars in globular clusters are some of the oldest stars in the galaxy, and by studying these stars scientists hope to determine the age of the universe.

PROJECT IDEA

The Pleiades is the best-known open cluster in the Milky Way galaxy, and people in both the Northern and Southern Hemispheres recognized it in the sky and told myths to explain its existence. In the Northern Hemisphere the Pleiades rose in the fall and signaled the onset of winter, so people in the Northern Hemisphere told myths of the Pleiades that emphasized its connection with hunger. In the Southern Hemisphere the Pleiades rose in the spring and announced the coming rains, so people in the Southern Hemisphere told myths that connected the star cluster to rain and flood.

The Pleiades contains about 100 stars, but only six or seven of them can be seen with the naked eye. In myths, the Pleiades has been known as seven sisters, seven brothers, a hen and six chicks, seven maidens, seven thieves, and seven hungry children. But sometimes early myth-makers could only see six stars in the star cluster, and they told myths to explain the missing star.

The Greeks explained the missing star in a myth about Merope, the daughter of Atlas. Atlas had seven daughters, but Merope was the only one of them who married a mortal. Zeus placed all seven of the sisters in the sky to shine as stars, but Merope was ashamed of her husband and hid her head.

The books below contain myths of the Pleiades. Discuss these myths with the class and then have students write myths of their own to explain the Pleiades. Their myths can explain how this star cluster got into the sky, they can explain how the star cluster signals the seasons, or they can explain why one of the seven stars in the cluster appears to be missing.

SUGGESTED READING

Allen, Richard Hinkley. *Star Names: Their Lore and Meaning.* New York: Dover, 1963.

Andrews, Tamra. *Legends of the Earth, Sea, and Sky: An Encyclopedia of Nature Myths.* Santa Barbara, CA: ABC-CLIO, 1998.

Krupp, E. C. *Beyond the Blue Horizon: Myths and Legends of the Sun, Moon, Stars, and Planets.* New York: Oxford University Press, 1991.

TOPIC 4. Star Maps

Star maps have taken different forms and have appeared on animal skins and in ancient tombs, on cave walls, and on celestial globes. People began mapping the heavens long ago when they felt a need to organize the many stars they saw glistening in the sky above them, but over the years star maps have evolved into works of art. Artists' renderings of star maps show the sky world as a mystical, magical place.

PROJECT IDEA

Have students choose one of the eighty-eight constellations developed by the ancient Greeks and read the myth the Greeks told to explain it. The best-known Greek constellation stories appear in *Phaenomena*, by Arastus of Soli, and in *Poeticon Astronomica*, by Hygenis, but these stories have been retold time and time again and appear in many different sources. Have students create a star map to place their constellation in the heavens. Have them connect the dots to form the picture in the myth, and have them label the bright stars. To map the constellation in the heavens students can draw the other constellations near it in the sky. The list of books and Web sites below is just a selection of the numerous sources available that will help students identify myths and design their star maps.

SUGGESTED READING

Lurie, Alison, and Monika Beisner. *The Heavenly Zoo: Legends and Tales of the Stars.* New York: Farrar, Straus and Giroux, 1996.

Contains myths and legends from around the world and has lots of illustrations.

McDonald, Marianne. *Mythology of the Zodiac: Tales of the Constellations.* Friedman/Fairfax, 2000.

Recounts and compares the tales of the zodiac from cultures around the globe. Has beautiful illustrations.

Raymo, Chet. *365 Starry Nights: An Introduction to Astronomy for Every Night of the Year.* New York: Simon & Schuster, 1982.

Includes information on each constellation and contains star maps.

Rey, H. A. *Find the Constellations.* Boston: Houghton Mifflin, 1976.

Contains information about how the stars formed, where they are located in the sky, and myths about each constellation. Contains interactive quizzes and star charts.

Ridpath, Ian. *Star Tales*. New York: Universe Books, 1988.

Written for young adults and covers the history of stargazing and the origin of each of the eighty-eight constellations in the night sky.

Sasaki, Chris. *The Constellations: Stars and Stories*. New York: Sterling, 2001.

Contains information and tips for stargazing as well as stories about all 88 constellations. Lots of illustrations and star charts, including charts for each season.

TOPIC 5.   Supernovas

Astronomers can now witness the birth and death of a star thanks to the astounding power of the Hubble Space Telescope. This telescope has allowed astronomers to observe the process of stellar evolution. Today's astronomers have seen the clouds of gas collapse and they have seen stars in each stage of their development, but many casual observers have actually seen supernova explosions with their naked eyes. A supernova that exploded in February 1987 was the brightest supernova observed in forty years. It was named Supernova 1987A and it appeared in the Large Magellanic Cloud, a galaxy that's visible in the southern sky near the Milky Way.

PROJECT IDEA

Read about Supernova 1987A and some of the famous supernovas in history. Then divide the class into two groups. Have one group of students prepare a report that explains what people long ago thought when they saw bright explosions in the sky. Have the other group explain what astronomers have since learned about supernovas. Have each group present their reports to the class.

SUGGESTED READING

Asimov, Isaac. *The Exploding Suns: The Secrets of Supernovas*. New York: Plume, 1996.

> Written for young adults. Provides the history of supernova observation and reaction, and contains an easily understood overview of the science of exploding stars.

Nicholson, Iain. *Stars and Supernovas*. New York: DK Publishing, 2001.

> Geared toward high school students but contains colorful photos, inserts, and clear explanations of star formation and supernovas that make the book readable for younger students too.

The zodiac we recognize today comes from ancient Greece but people in many other lands also had zodiacs. You might be familiar with the Chinese zodiac, which often appears on menus or placemats in Chinese restaurants. The Chinese zodiac consists of twelve animals, just like the Greek zodiac, but it's based on a twelve-year cycle rather than on a monthly cycle.

PROJECT IDEA

Have students check their Chinese zodiac signs in Table 3.3. Then read them stories about the Chinese zodiac from the books below. Have each student make a poster that compares their Greek zodiac sign with their Chinese zodiac sign. They can draw pictures of the characters from each zodiac, and they can compare the attributes and qualities the Greeks and the Chinese assigned to each sign.

TABLE 3.3 · The Chinese Zodiac

Animal	Dates
Rat	1948, 1960, 1972, 1984, 1996, 2008
Ox	1949, 1961, 1973, 1985, 1997, 2009
Tiger	1950, 1962, 1974, 1986, 1998, 2010
Hare	1951, 1963, 1975, 1987, 1999, 2011
Dragon	1952, 1964, 1976, 1988, 2000, 2012
Snake	1953, 1965, 1977, 1989, 2001, 2013
Horse	1954, 1966, 1978, 1990, 2002, 2014
Sheep	1955, 1967, 1979, 1991, 2003, 2015
Monkey	1956, 1968, 1980, 1992, 2004, 2016
Rooster	1957, 1969, 1981, 1993, 2005, 2017
Dog	1958, 1970, 1982, 1994, 2006, 2018
Boar	1959, 1971, 1983, 1995, 2007, 2019

SUGGESTED READING

Crawford, Gregory. *Animals in the Stars: Chinese Astrology for Children*. Rochester, VT: Inner Traditions Intl., Ltd., 2002.

Includes an introduction to Chinese astrology and uses myths and legends to provide information on the Chinese zodiac.

McDonald, Marianne. *Mythology of the Zodiac.* New York: Metro Books, 1999.

Compares myths of the zodiac from many lands. Includes lots of photographs and illustrations.

Whitfield, Susan. *The Legend of the Chinese Zodiac.* Cambridge, MA: Barefoot Books, 1998.

Retelling of a legend that explains the Chinese calendar.

—— SUGGESTED READING FOR TEACHERS

Allen, Richard Hinckley. *Star Names: Their Lore and Their Meaning*. New York: Dover, 1963.

> A classic book on star mythology. Contains history, etymology, and lore of the constellations.

Condos, Thoeny. *Star Myths of the Greeks and Romans: A Sourcebook Containing the Constellations of the Pseudo-Eratoshenes and the Poetic Astronomy of Hyginus*. Grand Rapids, MI: Phanes Press, 1997.

> Details and explains the constellation myths of the Greeks and Romans and contains numerous references to additional sources.

Devorkin, David, ed. *Beyond Earth: Mapping the Universe*. Washington, DC: National Geographic Society, 2002.

> Combines science with the myths and art of cultures around the globe.

Marschall, Laurence A. *The Supernova Story*. Princeton, NJ: Princeton University Press, 1994.

> Provides an explanation of Supernova 1987A as well as an overview of the history of supernovas.

Mitton, Jacqueline. *Once Upon a Starry Night: A Book of Constellation Stories*. Washington, DC: National Geographic Society, 2003.

> Contains facts and myths about stars, nebulae, galaxies, and constellations.

Ridpath, Ian. *Star Tales*. New York: Universe Books, 1988.

> Includes myths of the stars and constellations as well as the origin and history of the eighty-eight constellations designed by the Greeks that are recognized today.

Staal, Julius D. *The New Patterns in the Sky: Myths and Legends of the Stars*. Blacksburg, VA: McDonald & Woodward, 1988.

> Contains legends of the constellations from different countries.

4 .... The Planets

——————— THE MYTHS OF THE PLANETS

The planets seemed mysterious to ancient skywatchers. They looked like stars but they didn't remain fixed like stars; they wandered back and forth across the sky. The ancients recognized five planets—Mercury, Venus, Mars, Jupiter, and Saturn. Ancient people didn't know these objects were planets because they seemed like supernatural beings. They moved through the sky world like the Sun and the Moon, and they appeared to have wills of their own.

Venus enjoyed particular fame in early sky myths and often appeared in the stories as a beautiful goddess. Venus is the brightest planet, and people on Earth can see it clearly as it moves from the morning sky to the evening sky in regular cycles.

Read the following myth about Venus, the planet that people in much of the world worshipped as Morning Star. This myth is from Lithuania, and it shows how people in the Baltic lands worshipped their Morning Star as the daughter of the Sun.

"The Maiden of the Sea," a Myth from Lithuania

Long ago in Lithuania, all the people in the land worshipped the Sun as a beautiful goddess. This goddess brought light and heat to the world, and the people called her Saule. Saule smiled down on the people and gave them the gift of warmth when they were chilled and cold, and she restored the land to fruitfulness after the ice gods stole the leaves from the trees and froze the fields solid. Each spring, throughout the land, the people gathered together and sang songs to their goddess. They loved her dearly for shining so brightly on the land and for melting the snows that covered their world all winter long.

Saule was the most beautiful and the most radiant goddess in all the land, and the love the people felt for her was strong and their devotion to her faithful. Then one day, another goddess was born. She rose from the depths of the sea and brightened the world with her shiny golden hair. Some said this new goddess was Saule's own daughter and many agreed that this goddess was even more glorious than her mother. Joseph, a young man of the countryside had seen her long before anyone else had. He called her the second Sun, and he went out to search for her.

"I see two Suns in the sky now," Joseph said to his brothers. "One in the morning at breakfast and one in the evening at vespers. I must go and search for the second Sun."

Joseph's brothers looked at him strangely, for they saw only one Sun in the sky. They blessed their brother nevertheless, and they sent him on his way.

Joseph traveled through fields and forests, and he asked the animals to help him, for he thought they might lead him to the second Sun.

"I am searching for the second Sun," he told the animals. "She shines in the morning at breakfast and in the evening at vespers. Can you help me find her?"

"Go to the House of the Winds," the animals told him. "The Winds can help you find the Sun."

So Joseph traveled to the House of the Winds. There the North Wind, the South Wind, the East Wind, and the West Wind whirled around furiously as if they knew all the secrets of the universe.

"I am searching for the second Sun," Joseph told the Winds. "I see her in the morning at breakfast and in the evening at vespers. Can you tell me where to find her?"

"That is not the Sun you see," the North Wind replied. "I saw her myself. There is a maiden who lives on an island in the sea, in a palace. You must travel to the end of the forest and wait by the shore. The maiden has a herd of cattle on the island and in the evening they come to the forest to graze. Wait for the cattle, and ask them to take you to the maiden."

Joseph did what the Winds told him to do. He followed them through the forest to the edge of the sea and waited for evening. Sure enough, when the Sun sank below the horizon, the cattle came to the shore to graze. And sure enough, the cattle took him to the island. There he found the maiden sleeping. Her hair framed her face like golden rays of sunlight. There was no doubt that no lovelier a maiden had ever been born.

What happened after that was quite strange, for Joseph didn't have the heart to awaken the maiden and he simply asked the cattle to take him back to the shore, and they did. Perhaps Joseph wanted to keep the image of the maiden sleeping with him forever, or perhaps he was afraid to awaken her for fear of some magic spell. But Joseph had found the second Sun and he cut a lock of her hair to hold with him forever and remember his golden goddess. He put the lock of hair inside a seashell he found in the sand, and he carried it across the sea on the back of a bull.

Unfortunately for Joseph however, the waves were quite rough that day and they tossed him and tumbled him and made it quite difficult for the young man to hold onto the bull's neck. Joseph did manage to hold on, but he lost hold of the seashell. The waves ripped it from his hands and carried it to the bottom of the sea. By the time they reached shore, Joseph saw the reflection of the hair shining up through the waters. It was almost daylight and the glorious light sparkled in the morning twilight more radiant and beautiful than ever.

Now up until that time, Saule had ruled as the most radiant goddess, as she had from the beginning of time. And she continued to live in her golden sky palace and bring light and warmth to the world. But now there was another goddess more radiant than she, and this goddess transfixed all who gazed upon her as she shone gloriously over the waters. The people on Earth named the new goddess Ausrine and they sang songs to worship her. Meness, the Moon, fell in love with Ausrine, and he abandoned his affections for Saule who had always before lit his life with her glorious sunlight. Saule was insane with jealousy. She sank beneath the sea in shame and refused to rise for several days.

Some people believed that Ausrine was actually Saule's own daughter, for she had the same golden hair as the Sun and she shone just as brightly as the sun in the sky. Saule had five other beautiful daughters as well—Vaivora, Zemyna, Ziezdre, Selija, and Indraja—and all of them were bright and beautiful. But everyone agreed that none of them was as lovely as Ausrine. Her golden hair formed an aura of light that filled the world with magic, and she enchanted all who gazed upon her when she lit the sea and the sky.

There was no question that Ausrine was beautiful, and at times Saule hated her daughter for shining so brightly and for stealing the love of Meness the Moon, who had always loved Saule the most. Ausrine knew of her mother's jealously but she loved her nevertheless, and she vowed to stay faithful to her and remain by her side. Ausrine lit the palace fires for her mother each morning and she lit the palace fires for her again each night. She attended the horses that carried her mother across the sky in her golden chariot, and she continued to accompany her mother on her journey across the heavens. But at times Saule's jealousy got the better of her, and the Sun goddess dove into the sea each night for fear that Ausrine's light would outshine her. Often times Ausrine rose in the morning sky before the Sun goddess and glowed right through breakfast, and often times she began shining in the twilight at vespers, and remained in the sky long after her mother disappeared.

Ausrine lived with her mother in the sky, but sometimes she, too, dove into the sea, and she returned to her own palace on the island and she danced on a stone. The people sang songs to Ausrine and worshipped her. They loved her all the more for remaining faithful to her mother and they praised her loyalty to the Sun as they watched her on the beach making golden slippers for her mother and sewing her mother's shining skirts, weaving them lovingly and carefully with gold and silver stripes. Ausrine loved the beach and she loved her island palace, for she was born from the sea and had lived there long before she rose to the sky. Still today the people love to watch her dance. Each year on Easter and on the first day of summer Ausrine dances for them. The people gather by the sea and they watch her dancing on the stone, her rays of light rippling through the water and shining up to the sky as she moves and sways.

· ·

"The Maiden of the Sea" was adapted—quite a bit so—from an account of an original legend published in *Of Gods and Men: Studies in Lithuanian Mythology*, by Algirdas J. Greimas (Indianapolis: Indiana University Press, 1992), and from a number of secondary sources that appear in the Suggested Reading sections below.

THE SCIENCE OF THE PLANETS

Planets exhibit curious behavior in the sky world. Unlike stars, they wander. They move back and forth from east to west and they appear in a different place in the sky every night. Skywatchers of the ancient world paid close attention to the stars, and they made no distinction between stars and planets. But they did notice that certain bright objects behaved differently than others. Venus and Mars exhibited the most obvious movements, but Venus shone brightest in the sky.

The Lithuanians were not the only group of people to worship the Morning Star as a beautiful goddess. The chapter on meteors tells how the Pawnee of North America worshiped Mars as the Morning Star, but most people gave this honor to Venus. The Babylonians called Venus Ishtar or Inanna, and the Romans made her their goddess of love.

BELIEF: The Sun is the mother of all the planets.

In "The Maiden of the Sea," Saule, the Sun goddess, was the mother of Ausrine. Other Lithuanian myths name Saule as the mother of two children, Ausrine, the Morning Star, and Wakarine, the Evening Star. Still other myths name Saule as the mother of all the planets: Ausrine (Venus,) Vaivora (Mercury), Zemyna (Earth), Ziezdre (Mars), Selija (Saturn), and Indraja (Jupiter). Of course, Ausrine and Wakarine were both the same planet, which looked like one goddess when she shone in the morning dawn and another when she shone in the evening twilight. The people who worshipped Venus had much to learn about the motion of the heavens, but long before scientists explained these motions ancient people tracked the travels of Venus across the sky.

In "The Maiden of the Sea," Ausrine appeared to be Saule's daughter because these two bright celestials appeared to move and light the sky together. But the Sun is a star and Venus is a planet. They're two very different kinds of celestial bodies though they both formed about four and a half billion years ago from a cloud of interstellar dust. Stars shine by themselves, and the Sun, like every other star, is a burning ball of gas. Venus and the other planets get their light from the Sun, however, and so does the Moon.

BELIEF: The brightness of Venus rivals that of the Sun.

Venus is clearly the brightest object in the sky next to the Sun and the Moon. Venus is so bright because it's so close to Earth but also because it's surrounded by clouds that reflect the Sun's light. Venus is so bright in the morning and evening because its orbit around the Sun takes it into the sky before the Sun rises at some times of year and allows it to remain in the sky after the Sun sets at other times. People in cold lands felt particularly awed by bright celestials, and they worshipped the Sun for renewing the Earth and for rescuing them from the winter cold. For this reason the Lithuanians worshipped Venus, as well as the Sun, as a powerful goddess. Ausrine and Saule both had the power to light their world and bathe the Earth with a soft, warm glow. Venus is so bright that it easily reflects enough light to outshine the stars, but it can't drown out other sky objects, and it certainly can't overpower the Sun. Venus can be seen in the daytime however, if the Sun is not too bright and if skywatchers know where to look. But it's difficult to see Venus with the bright Sun shining so close to it. The Sun is most definitely the brightest object in the heavens.

BELIEF: Venus is different from the other stars in the sky.

Most myths of the planets centered around Venus because, aside from the Sun and Moon, Venus is the most easily recognized celestial body. Many people mistake Venus for a star, but it's the second planet from the Sun and Earth's nearest neighbor. Today we recognize nine planets, but only five are visible to the naked eye—Mercury, Venus, Mars, Jupiter, and Saturn. From our position on Earth, these five bodies shine like the stars, but they're not stars at all. Planets are much smaller than stars, and while stars shine with their own light, planets don't. Many groups of people in early times recognized these celestial bodies, but they didn't recognize their own Earth as one of the same objects. And they didn't know that Uranus, Neptune, and Pluto existed at all until after the invention of the telescope in the sixteenth century.

Mercury, Venus, and Mars are called *terrestrial planets* because they're similar to the Earth in structure. All four of these planets formed at the same time and from the same rocky space debris. So did the Earth's moon. All of these bodies are heavily cratered. These four terrestrial planets are all small and heavy compared to the other planets because they're composed of rock and metal. Venus is the most similar to the Earth in both size and density, which is why scientists often call it Earth's twin. Because all of the inner planets were much closer together when they first formed than they are today, they had even more similarities in the beginning of their lives than they do now.

Jupiter, Saturn, Uranus, and Neptune are much different from the inner planets because they're not made of rock and metal; they're composed primarily of gas. Scientists call these outer planets "gas giants," which refers both to their composition and to their size. Jupiter, Saturn, Uranus, and Neptune are huge compared to the other planets, and Jupiter is the largest of them all. The size of Jupiter makes it easy to observe with a good pair of binoculars. Early skywatchers had no trouble seeing Mercury, Venus, and Mars, but those who paid close attention to the movements of the heavens could see Jupiter even without binoculars. They could see Saturn too, and those who watched closely recognized it as one of five celestials that moved differently from the rest. The discovery of Uranus and Neptune came much later, after the invention of the telescope. Telescopes paved the way for scientists to unravel many mysteries of the universe, and to discover that another planet lay far beyond the planet Neptune. In 1930 a man named Clyde Tombaugh discovered Pluto, the smallest of all the planets discovered so far. Pluto lies in the far reaches of the solar system where it's so far from the Sun's light that it remains dark and cold.

TABLE 4.1 · Characteristics of the Planets

Planet	Avg. Temp.	Orbit	Axis	Distance from Sun (in million miles)	Diameter (in miles)
Mercury (messenger god)	870−−300°F	88 days	176 days	36	3,030
Venus (goddess of love and beauty)	900°F	225 days	243 days	67	7,700
Earth	45°F	365¼ days	24 hours	93	7,926
Mars (god of war)	−190−90°F	687 days	24 hours, 37 min.	142	4,212
Jupiter (ruler of the sky)	−244°F	12 years	10 hours	483	88,846
Saturn (god of time)	−300°F	29 years	11 hours	888	74,898
Uranus (god of the starry sky)	−350°F	84 years	17 hours	1,784	31,763
Neptune (god of the sea)	−370°F	165 years	16 hour	2,794	31,000
Pluto (god of the underworld)	−390°F	248 years	6 days	3,647	1,485

··

BELIEF: Venus moves across the sky.

While ancient people paid close attention to the movements of the heavens they noticed that certain objects moved back and forth across the background of stars. When Galileo looked through his telescope, he could tell for certain how the planets move. The planets move in orbits around the Sun. Each planet stays in its own orbit, and each moves at its own speed. All of the planets travel along the imaginary plane of the ecliptic, and they complete their travels in set time periods. Mercury and Venus travel along the ecliptic in orbits closer to the Sun than the Earth, and the other planets travel in orbits outside the Earth. Therefore, from our position on Earth, Mercury and Venus have much different sky patterns than the other planets.

··

BELIEF: Venus always moves across the sky with the Sun.

It takes Venus 225 days to orbit the Sun, and in that time it makes the cycle from Morning Star, when it appears in the sky just before sunrise, to Evening Star, when it appears in the sky just after sunset, and back to Morning Star again. Mercury completes this same cycle only much faster, and from Earth the movement of Mercury is not nearly as noticeable as the movement of Venus. Because Mercury and Venus move inside the orbit of the Earth, they always move with the Sun. That's why in "The Maiden of the Sea" Ausrine remains ever faithful to her mother. Ausrine always follows Saule on her journeys because Venus always follows the Sun across the sky.

There are two times in the cycle of Venus when the planet appears in conjunction with the Sun. This means that Venus is so close to the Sun that skywatchers can't see the planet at all. The Sun's light out-shines it completely. Venus travels with the Sun for a while, then its path takes it farther away from the Sun and a little to the east of it. Venus is so bright that it's still possible to see it in the daytime if you know where to look. But most people can't see Venus in the daytime sky at all during this time. They see it in the evening and it remains on the western horizon after the Sun sets. Venus shines so brightly in the evening that skywatchers of times past considered it their bright sky goddess who announced the coming of night. When the Sun sinks below the horizon, Venus continues to light the night. That's why the myths say that Saule dives into the sea or sinks under the horizon and hides her head in shame.

As Venus continues on its path along the ecliptic, it moves a little higher in the sky each night. The planet climbs higher and higher in the sky and it remains as the illustrious Evening Star for a while before it turns around and moves west. Venus gets closer and closer to the Sun until once again the Sun drowns out the planet's light. Then Venus disappears for a while. It rises in the east before the Sun, making it the Morning Star and the goddess of dawn. Venus lights the morning dawn for a while, and then it turns around again. Then it moves closer to the Sun until the Sun's light outshines it once more. But the planet keeps moving. It disappears again before it reappears again as Evening Star. Venus, and the planet Mercury as well, always follow the Sun across the sky.

BELIEF: Venus changes as it moves in the sky.

Because the Earth and the other planets orbit the Sun, the planets appear in a different place in the sky every night. Venus shines brightly in both the morning and the evening, so ancient myths about Venus often named this bright celestial as two separate goddesses. The Lithuanians were not the only ones to call the Morning Star and the Evening Star two sisters; people from other countries told similar tales. Mayan myths about Venus identified the planet as Hero Twins. The movement of Venus was so obvious to astute skywatchers that the ancient Maya made elaborate Venus tables to keep track of time.

Because the orbit of Venus is inside the orbit of Earth, it is called an *inferior planet*. So is Mercury. Mars, Jupiter, Saturn, Uranus, Neptune, and Pluto have orbits outside the orbit of Earth and are called *superior planets*. The inferior planets always move in and out of the Sun's light as they move in the sky. Because Venus and Mercury always move in and out of the Sun's light, observers on Earth see Mercury and Venus go through phases like the Moon. It's hard to see the phases of Venus with the naked eye, but observers can see the phases of Venus clearly with a telescope. Look at Figure 4.1, which shows the orbit of Venus. When the Sun, the Earth, and Venus are in conjunction with the Sun but in alignment with the Earth, observers on Earth see Venus

FIGURE 4.1 · The Orbit of Venus

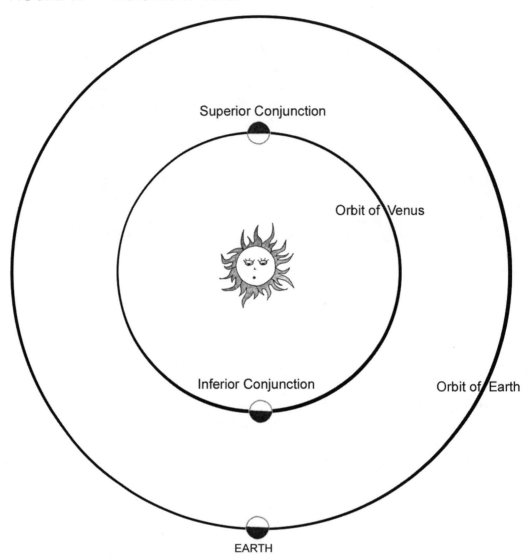

in either its full phase or its new phase. At superior conjunction, when Venus is on the far side of the Sun from Earth, we see the planet in its full phase. At inferior conjunction, when Venus is on the near side of the Sun from Earth, the planet is in its new phase and we don't see it at all.

— TOPICS FOR DISCUSSION AND PROJECTS

TOPIC 1. Songs to the Morning Star

The people in the myth sang songs to both the Sun goddess and the Morning Star. These Lithuanian folk songs were called *dainos* and they served as a form of worship of the bright celestials that brought light to their world. The Lithuanians had a symbol for the Sun and for Ausrine—an eight-pointed star—which the Baltic peoples considered a symbol of good luck. They wore it on their clothes, and they carved it into their swords and on the bridles of their horses. The Balts placed the star symbol on their horses' bridles to indicate the connection between Ausrine and the solar horse, the animal who carried the Sun across the sky.

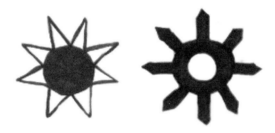

PROJECT IDEA

Have students write a song or poem to honor the Morning Star. They can use colored paper to frame their poem and paint a symbol of the morning star on their paper. The suggested readings below will help students write poems and identify star motifs to decorate their papers.

SUGGESTED READING

Bruce-Mitford, Miranda. *Illustrated Book of Signs and Symbols*. Mineola, NY: Dover, 1996.

Contains color illustrations of signs and symbols in nature and in other subject areas. Includes symbols of the Sun.

Fletcher, Ralph. *Poetry Matters: Writing a Poem from the Inside Out*. New York: HarperTrophy, 2002.

Discusses how to convey feelings and images in poems and emphasizes wordplay over rhyme. Discusses how to recite poetry aloud. Includes interviews with children's poets.

Hulme, Joy. *How to Write, Recite, and Delight in All Kinds of Poetry*. Brookfield, CT: Millbrook Press, 2003.

Provides a clear lesson in creative writing to help students read, write, understand, and recite poetry.

Nye, Naomi. *This Same Sky: A Collection of Poems from Around the World*. New York: Greenwillow, 2000.

Contains contemporary poems from sixty-eight countries around the world.

TOPIC 2. Symbolism of the Planets

The Lithuanians were certainly not the only ones to personify the planets and name them as gods. The ancient Chinese personified the planets and they identified them with the five elements they considered active forces in the universe. The Chinese identified Jupiter with wood, Mars with fire, Saturn with Earth, Venus with metal, and Mercury with water. Over the years Western astrology has linked the planets with certain symbols. Each of the planets was connected with a metal, a color, a stone, and an animal. These symbols and associations applied to the Sun and the Moon and the five planets recognized by early sky-watchers.

PROJECT IDEA

Tell students to choose one of the planets listed below and create their own symbol for the planet based on its physical characteristics. They might choose an animal for their symbol, or they might choose a stone. They can create their planet symbol out of clay or papier-mâché. Then they can use appropriate colors and motifs to reflect the physical characteristics of their planet or the myth connected with it. The books in the Suggested Reading section below will help students gain an understanding of each planet's characteristics, and the books on clay models and papier-mâché will help them design their projects.

> **Mercury**—Mercury's metal is quicksilver, the mercury now used in thermometers. Its color is gray, its stone is an agate, and its animal is a swallow that flies quickly in the sky, just like the quickest of all planets.
>
> **Venus**—Venus is associated with bright, shiny copper and with the color green. Its stone is the green emerald and its animal is another bird, the dove.
>
> **Mars**—Mars is associated with iron and also with the color red, because red is the color of the soil on Mars. Its stone is the red ruby and its animal is the horse.
>
> **Jupiter**—Jupiter's metal is tin and its color is blue. The stone that symbolizes Jupiter is the sapphire and the animal is the eagle.
>
> **Saturn**—Saturn is connected with lead and the color black. Its stone is a black onyx and its animal is the crocodile.

SUGGESTED READING

Schwartz, Renée F. *Papier-Mâché*. Toronto: Kids Can Press, 2000.

Includes eleven projects and lots of tips for making successful papier-mâché projects.

Seix, Victoria. *Creating with Papier-Mâché*. Farmington Hills, MI: Blackbirch Press, 2000.

Contains fifteen projects and instructions for creating with paper strips and paper pulp.

TOPIC 3. The Planets and the Gods

The planets were named after Roman gods for a reason. As astronomers in ancient times observed these planets they chose appropriate names for each one based on their movements and characteristics.

PROJECT IDEA

Have students choose one of the planets listed below and relate the myths of that planet to the class. The list below of the nine planets explains their connection to Roman myths, but there are myths of the planets from many other cultures as well.

> **Mercury**—Named after the Roman messenger god because of the planet's swift motion around the Sun.
>
> **Venus**—Named after the Roman goddess of love and beauty because the planet lights the morning and the evening skies with a beautiful bright light.
>
> **Mars**—Named after the Roman god of war because the red color of the planet reminded astronomers of blood.
>
> **Jupiter**—Named after the Roman sky god, the king of all the gods, because it is the largest planet.
>
> **Saturn**—Named after the Roman god of time because it was once believed to be on the outer reaches of the solar system.
>
> **Uranus**—Named after the Roman god of the starry sky.
>
> **Neptune**—Named after the god of the sea.
>
> **Pluto**—Named after the Roman god of the underworld because the planet resides in the darkest region of the solar system.

SUGGESTED READING

Evert, Laura. *Planets, Moons, and Stars.* Chanhassen, MN: Creative Publishing Intl., 2003.

> Introductory book on the solar system with lots of science, history, and legends of the planets.

Kid's Cosmos. "Planet Myths and Lore." *http://www.kidscosmos.org/kid-stuff/planet-lore-5.html#moons*

> Contains brief recaps of the myths related to names of the planets and their moons' names, and scientific facts about each planet and moon.

Scientists used to believe that only Saturn had rings, but now they know that all the gas giants have them. The rings of Uranus were discovered in 1977, and this discovery led to the knowledge that Jupiter and Neptune have rings, too. Saturn has the brightest rings of all the planets, and Saturn's rings are made of ice. But the rings of the other planets are equally amazing. Planetary rings appear to contain debris from comets or asteroids that collided with the planet or the planet's moons long ago.

PROJECT IDEA

Divide your class into four groups. Have each group create a poster of one of the four gas giants that shows its rings. Students can include on the poster a short report that explains the formation of planetary rings.

SUGGESTED READING

Evert, Laura. *Planets, Moons, and Stars*. Chanhassen, MN: Creative Publishing Intl., 2003.

> Introductory book on the solar system with lots of science, history, and legends of the planets.

Henbest, Nigel, and Heather Couper. *DK Space Encyclopedia*. New York: DK Publishing, 1999.

> Contains lots of color photographs and clear explanations of the planets and their rings.

TOPIC 5. Planetary Moons

Except for Mercury and Venus, all of the planets in the solar system have moons. The Earth has only one moon, but Uranus and Saturn have many. New moons were discovered around these planets as recently as 2003. Moons are called natural satellites because they revolve around their planets in natural orbits. All the moons in the solar system have been named after characters from Greek and Roman myths and literature.

PROJECT IDEA

Divide the class into six groups, one for each planet (other than Earth) that has moons. Have each group make a mural to describe the moons of their planet. The mural could include information on the mythological characters for which both the planets and the moons were named, and it could include diagrams of the planets and the orbits of the moons. It could also include factual information about the planets and the moons. The books in the Suggested Reading section will help students explain facts and identify myths for all the moons in the solar system, and the image catalog and photo gallery on NASA's National Space Science Data Center Web site will help them create pictures and diagrams of the planets and their moons.

The Moons of Mars

Phobos
Deimos

The Moons of Jupiter

Europa
Ganymede
Callisto
Io
Metis
Adrastea
Amalthea
Thebe
Leda
Himalia
Lysithea
Elara
Ananke
Carme

Pasiphae
Sinope

The Named Moons of Saturn

Pan
Atlas
Prometheus
Pandora
Epimetheus
Janus
Mimas
Enceladus
Tethys
Telesto
Calypso
Dione
Helene
Rhea
Titan

Hyperion	Bianca
Iapetus	Ophelia
Phoebe	Cordelia

The Named Moons of Uranus	**The Named Moons of Neptune**
Oberon	
Titania	Triton
Umbriel	Nereid
Ariel	Proteus
Miranda	Larissa
Juliet	Galatea
Portia	Despina
Rosalind	Thalassa
Belinda	Naiad
Puck	
Desdemona	**The Moons of Pluto**
Cressida	Charon

SUGGESTED READING

Henbest, Nigel, and Heather Couper. *DK Space Encyclopedia*. New York: DK Publishing, 1999.

> Contains lots of color photos and clear explanations of the planets and their moons.

Kid's Cosmos. "Planet Myths and Lore." *Kid's Cosmos. http://www.kidscosmos.org/kid-stuff.*

> Click on planet lore to access brief recaps of the myths related to names of the planets and their moons. This site also contains scientific facts about each planet and moon.

NASA. "National Space Science Data Center." *http://nssdc.gsfc.nasa.gov. http://nssdc. gsfc.nas.gov/photo_gallery.*

> NASA's Space Science Data Center Web site contains an image catalog and photo gallery.

TOPIC 6. The Discovery of Pluto

Pluto is the ninth planet of the solar system, but some scientists question whether it should be labeled a planet at all. It's so small that it might just be another icy body similar to a comet that orbits around the Sun in an outer area of the solar system. Pluto is so far away that scientists have yet to unravel many of its mysteries.

PROJECT IDEA

Have students write a report on the discovery of Pluto. Their report should consist of two parts: One part should include information on what scientists have learned about our ninth planet; the second part should discuss the possibility of locating a tenth planet in the solar system.

SUGGESTED READING

Asimov, Isaac. *How Did We Find Out about Pluto?* New York: Walker & Co., 1991.

> Discusses the search for Pluto as well as the possibility of discovering a tenth planet.

Cole, Michael D. *Pluto: The Ninth Planet.* Berkeley Heights, NJ: Enslow, 2002.

> Discusses events leading to the discovery of Pluto and contains information about the planet's atmosphere and composition.

Vogt, Gregory. *Pluto and the Search for New Planets.* New York: Raintree Steck-Vaughn, 2000.

> Covers the discovery of Pluto and gives information on how scientists search for new planets in the solar system.

—— SUGGESTED READING FOR TEACHERS

Asimov, Isaac. *Venus, Near Neighbor to the Sun*. New York: Lothrop, Lee, and Shepherd, 1981.

> Includes information on the Morning Star and Evening Star phenomena, a comparison of Venus to other planets, an explanation of the phases of Venus, and lots of maps.

Gribben, John, and John Goodwin. *Empire of the Sun: Planets and Moons of the Solar System*. New York: New York University Press, 1998.

> Contains a detailed introduction to the planets, their moons and rings, as well as comets and other bodies in the solar system. Includes lots of illustrations, including some of the planets and their moons and rings.

Krupp, E. C. *Beyond the Blue Horizon: Myths and Legends of the Sun, Moon, Stars, and Planets*. New York: Oxford University Press, 1991.

> The chapter called "By the Light of the Morning Star" provides a clear explanation of the movements of the planets and the phenomena of Morning Star and Evening Star. It also explains Venus's role in the myths of many cultures.

5 ············ The Milky Way Galaxy

─────── THE MYTHS OF THE MILKY WAY

The sky was so dark in the ancient world that the Milky Way looked like a glistening white band streaking from horizon to horizon. Some people called it a river, some called it a path of spilled milk, and some called it a sparkling road, a road lit by heavenly fires that guided people from one world to the next. Early skywatchers offered many explanations for the bright band they saw spanning the heavens. Because they envisioned the sky as a magical land, they connected the Milky Way with the sparkling lights of godly palaces. Because the band appeared to lead from one part of the sky to another, it seemed logical that it served as a path. Whether river or stream, bridge or road, early myth-makers believed the Milky Way led travelers to another world. It helped explain how the celestial deities traveled across the sky, and it helped explain how souls of the dead traveled to heaven.

People who felt awed by celestial phenomena found the Milky Way particularly impressive. And it looked different in the Southern Hemisphere than it did in the north. The Andes Mountains lie south of the equator, and the Inca of Peru believed that the Andean empire was governed by the Milky Way and by the stars around it. They believed that their empire began in 200 B.C. when the Sun first rose over the Milky Way and that the empire ended in 1532 when the Sun failed to do so.

The following story was adapted from ancient Peruvian myths that stressed the role of the Milky Way as both a celestial river and a crucial player in the water cycle. Read the story and learn how the ancient

Peruvians viewed the Milky Way. Then use The Science of the Milky Way section to learn facts about our galaxy and about the other galaxies in the universe.

"Yacana the Llama and the Secret of Rain," a Myth from Peru

High above the mountains, on a dark night long ago, the animals moved in the sky. They moved along the banks of a great white river that stretched from horizon to horizon, and some played a game of chase through the waters of heaven. The people who lived in the mountains knew the sky animals well because they saw them moving when they gazed into the night. When the sky animals moved, they sent messages to the people, and they gazed down on the animals that walked the earth and looked after them.

The animals that lived in the sky long ago continue to live there today, though not everyone can see them moving. Sadly, not everyone can see the river either, for the nights now are so bright with city lights that the marvels of the sky world fade from view. But if no city lights drowned the heavens, people in much of the world could see that a river arches across the heavens, as thick and white as fresh milk. People fortunate enough to live close to the equator can see the animals—Yacana the llama and her young baby, Hanpatu the toad, Yutu the partridge, Atoq the fox, and Machacuay the rainbow snake. These animals make magic happen in the world every night. But it's much harder to recognize magic these days than it used to be.

Long ago the Inca who lived in the mountains of Peru recognized magic. They saw the river and the animals, and they learned to read the messages the animals sent them. The Inca built a magnificent empire in and around the city of Cuzco and they built temples to the Sun and to the other gods of the sky. In the Inca empire, the Sun ruled supreme, and everyone knew that magic existed in the celestial sphere.

The Inca empire grew to be the largest and greatest empire in all the world, stretching far across Peru and into current day Bolivia and Ecuador. Then the conquistadors came from across the sea and destroyed the great empire. Intent on converting the Inca to Christianity, they destroyed a lot of magic when they toppled the temples. The magic still exists, of course, but it's buried in secret places that not everyone can find. The sky animals continue to send messages to the people, but almost no one who lives in Peruvian cities today knows how to recognize the messages when they receive them.

They say that there are some people today who still recognize messages from the sky animals, and they say that there is a man who lives in a small village in the mountains who knows the secret of rain. It had been raining a long time when a young boy set out to find this man. The boy lived in a village at the foot of the mountains, and many of the houses in his village had been nearly destroyed by the rains already.

One day the boy set out on his journey up the mountain to find the man who knew the secret of rain. It was a long climb but he found the village. It wasn't long after he arrived that someone led him to the man who had answers no one else knew how to find.

"Can you tell me the secret of rain?" the boy asked the old man, who was sitting outside on a bench by his home.

The old man stood up and started walking, and he asked the boy to follow along. The man had a great herd of llamas, and he took the boy to see them. The llamas looked very strange. The entire herd lay in the fields and stared into the sky.

"They have been watching the sky every night for quite some time," the man said. "And they have refused to eat in the daytime for quite some time also. We must take heed of their behavior, for they are guided by the stars. We must watch the stars too, and we must watch Yacana."

The boy looked at the sky, and he looked at the llamas, and as the man turned away from the herds and headed back to his home the boy followed. The man returned to his bench outside under a tree, and the boy sat beside him on a branch that had fallen to the ground. He listened intently as the old man spoke his wisdom, and together they watched the sky grow dark.

"There is a great white river that flows through the sky," the man said. "And many months ago, Machacuay the rainbow snake rose from the river and brought the rain when he came. But we needed it then. You remember, now, don't you, how dry it was a while back? But when Machacuay came, the rains poured from the sky and turned the dry land green and lush again. Then the snakes came. We could see them crawling on the earth. This was a good thing," the man said.

He was quiet for a minute, and then he raised his eyebrows. "But now we must watch Yacana," he continued. "We will see her very soon, dipping her head into the river." The old man looked at the sky.

The boy looked at the sky too, but he did not yet understand.

"Who is Yacana?" the boy asked. "Is she in the sky?"

"Yes," the man said. "Yacana is in the sky. Yacana is a big black mama llama, and you will see her two bright eyes and her long neck. Then, if you look carefully, you will see her baby. The baby will be suckling. Stay with me here and we will watch the two of them move through the sky."

The man paused for a moment and watched the boy intently, to make sure he was listening.

"Yacana will drink from the great river," the man told the boy. "Then at midnight she will disappear, and the rains will stop."

"How do you know this?" the boy asked.

"The animals know," the man replied. "So we must watch them carefully."

"When will I see her?" the boy asked, his eyes wide with wonder. He wasn't sure he wanted the llama to come out of the sky in the dark. And he wasn't sure he would recognize her when she did.

"First you will see Atoq," the old man said. "Atoq is a fox. Then you will see Hanpatu the toad and Yutu the partridge. Then you will see Yacana."

"And Yacana will stop the rain?" the boy asked.

"Yes," the man said. "Yacana will stop the rain."

The old man stopped talking for a while and stared silently into the sky. The rains had ceased for a while, but the boy knew that it was just a matter of time before they would begin again. It was growing darker and darker, and the man continued to watch the sky. So the boy leaned back on the tree and watched the sky too. If this man was truly as wise as everyone said he was, the boy thought, Atoq the fox would soon appear, and then Hanpatu the toad and Yutu the partridge, and then Yacana with her baby. And then, if this man was truly as wise as everyone said he was, Yacana would come down from the sky and the rains would stop.

Sure enough, as the sky got darker, the boy saw the river. And to his amazement he saw Atoq the fox and Hanaptu the toad and Yutu the partridge, and then Yacana and her baby. The baby was suckling, and the animals moved along the great white river in the sky. Yacana dipped her head into the river and began to drink. Then around midnight, she disappeared, just as the man had said.

"It's true!" the boy said. "You do know the secret of rain!"

The old man smiled. "It is the animals who know the secret," he said. "And I have come to know the animals."

The boy sat and listened to the man for a long time, until long after Yacana disappeared and into the morning when the bright Sun rose in the sky and dried the fields. The boy had seen the animals in the sky, and soon he would learn to read their messages.

The man told the boy lots of stories of the sky animals, stories of Yacana and her baby, and stories of Machacuay the rainbow snake. He told the boy stories of Atoq the fox, and of Yutu the partridge, and he told the boy stories of how Yutu chases the toad through the sky but never catches him. The man taught the boy how to watch the animals on Earth, and how to recognize the secrets of the sky.

It was true that some people still know how to read messages in the sky, and because the man told his stories, the boy would know too, and he would pass the stories on. He thanked the man for revealing his secrets, and he watched the man as he walked slowly and silently to the fields to see his llamas. Then the boy headed down the mountain. The Sun was shining brightly. When he got home, he would tell his mother and all the other people in his village that the rains had stopped for a while, and that Yacana had saved the Earth from flooding. And he would tell them that when the Earth got dry the rains would come again, as soon as Machacuay the rainbow snake rose into the sky.

....

"Yacana the Llama and the Secret of Rain" is based on myths from ancient Peru that appear in *Astronomy and Empire in the Ancient Andes*, by Brian S. Bauer and David S. Dearborn (Austin: University of Texas Press, 1995), in *At the Crossroads of Earth and Sky*, by Gary Urton (Austin: University of Texas Press, 1999), and in *The Secret of the Incas: Myth, Astronomy, and the War Against Time*, by William Sullivan (New York: Crown, 1999).

THE SCIENCE OF THE MILKY WAY

When the conquistadors came from Spain and conquered the Inca empire, they couldn't see the dark cloud animals the natives saw in the sky. That's because you have to use your imagination to see them. Perhaps someone has to tell you they are there. That's what constellations are about. They're figments of the imagination. So are the dark cloud constellations, and so is the river in the sky.

....

BELIEF: The Milky Way spans the sky from one end to the other.

We learned in previous chapters that early people often viewed the sky world as a mirror image of their own world. They believed that the same forces that shaped their lives on Earth shaped the lives of the gods in heaven. The Peruvians considered their Vilacanota River an earthly reflection of the Milky Way, or as some say, a branch of the same river.

On Earth it runs from the southeast to the northwest, and in the sky it appears to extend from horizon to horizon.

It took scientists a long time before they identified the milky river that spanned the heavens as a galaxy. But the Inca didn't need to identify it to observe its movement. They simply used their eyes. And they told myths to assign significance to what they saw. The Huarochiri Manuscript survived destruction by the conquistadors and it serves as an important relic of pre-Columbian culture. This manuscript is written in Quechua, a native language of the Andean people, and it provides a wealth of information about the dark cloud constellations as well as other astronomical phenomena the Inca recognized.

Many people today never have an opportunity to see the Milky Way because they live in the city where bright lights overpower it. The Inca saw the great white river in the sky, however. They saw it so clearly because people in the Southern Hemisphere can see the center of the galaxy. In the Northern Hemisphere we can see only the outer edge.

The Milky Way is simply one of billions of galaxies in the universe. Each of those galaxies consists of billions of stars as well as dust, gas, planets, and asteroids. All of these bodies float in the atmosphere and are held together by gravity. Until the 1600s it was common to think of the Milky Way as a river because it looked like a long path of spilled milk that extended from horizon to horizon. But in 1610 Galileo looked through his telescope and saw the stars. Then, over time, other scientists unraveled more and more of our galaxy's mysteries.

Astronomers classify galaxies by shape, and the Milky Way looks nothing like a long path. The Milky Way is a spiral galaxy, and spiral galaxies are actually flat disks with spiral arms that swirl around the disks like a pinwheel. Our solar system lies in one of the spiral arms of the Milky Way, so when we look at the galaxy from the Northern Hemisphere we are actually seeing just one of its arms. This is the Orion arm. It got its name because it contains the constellation Orion, one of the most easily recognizable constellations in the night sky.

Look at the diagrams of the Milky Way galaxy in Figure 5.1. The side view shows that spiral galaxies look like flat disks with bulges in the centers. The most massive stars are inside the bulge, and outside the bulge the stars spread out. Most of the stars are located in the spiral arms. These are the areas where new stars are born. Look at the diagram that shows the spiral structure of the galaxy. You can't tell from the diagram, but if you look at photographs of the Milky Way you can see that the spiral arms look brighter than the rest of the disk. That's because newborn stars are often very hot and very bright.

FIGURE 5.1 · The Milky Way Galaxy

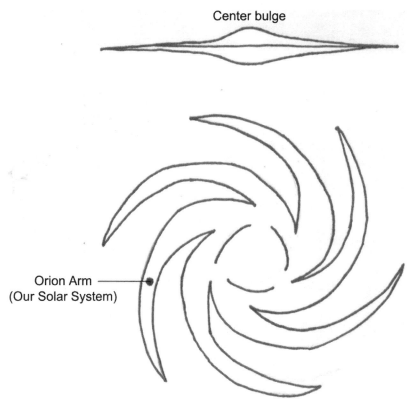

Center bulge

Orion Arm
(Our Solar System)

Three primary types of galaxies make up the universe: *spiral galaxies,* *elliptical galaxies,* and *irregular galaxies.* Spiral galaxies look like pinwheels, and they contain old stars in the center bulge and new stars in the spiral arms. Elliptical galaxies look like footballs or eggs, and they contain only old stars. The largest galaxies in the universe are elliptical galaxies, and some of them contain more than a trillion stars. Irregular galaxies have no identifiable form at all because the stars, gas, and dust are spread out randomly within them. The smallest galaxies in the universe are irregular galaxies, and some of them contain only a million stars.

When we look into the sky, all the stars we see are part of our own galaxy. From time immemorial people told stories of the stars and connected the points of light they saw to create images. The star-to-star constellations form like dot-to-dot pictures, and in between those pictures lie clouds of interstellar dust.

BELIEF: There are dark clouds in the Milky Way.

The sky looks much different in the Southern Hemisphere than it does in the north. People in both hemispheres can see the stars, but people in the Southern Hemisphere can also see the spaces between them. The Milky Way is particularly prominent in the Peruvian sky, and on dark nights people can see the spaces between the stars very clearly. From the Peruvian highlands, skywatchers who look at the Milky Way see black clouds in the southern half of the galaxy, and they make pictures or constellations out of these dark clouds just like people all over the world make constellations out of the stars. In the northern sky, it's hard to see the dark clouds, but in the southern sky there are a lot of them. People in Africa and the South Pacific can see these clouds too, and so can people in other parts of South America.

These dark clouds are called *nebulae*, and they're located in the densest part of the Milky Way where, in sharp contrast to the thick areas of bright stars, they look like silhouettes against a white river. The word nebula means cloud. Nebulae are simply large clouds of dust and gas, and they're composed primarily of nitrogen. Some astronomers have called nebulae "stellar nurseries" because in many of these clouds new stars are born.

Most nebulae are difficult to see with the naked eye, but they're absolutely beautiful when seen through powerful telescopes. Early people saw much more without telescopes than we can possibly imagine today, in part because the sky was so dark in the ancient world and in part because early farming people used the movements of the sky to understand the seasons on Earth. Dark nebulae like the ones the Inca identified are composed of dense dust and have no stars inside them or close around them at all. Planetary nebulae form when the outer layer of gas has blown off old stars, and supernova nebulae are the remnants of very massive stars that exploded many years earlier.

BELIEF: The dark clouds in the Milky Way have
identifiable shapes.

Because the Inca identified clear shapes in the dark patches of the Milky Way, they spun myths that helped them make sense of the sky.

The dark cloud animal they identified as a partridge, or a *tinamou*, is the closest nebula to the center of the Milky Way, and it's the easiest to see. Most people know it as the Coal Sack Nebula, but the Inca called it Yutu. The Coal Sack is a classic example of a dark nebula. The dark nebula just west of Yutu they called Hanaptu and they identified it as a toad. The dark cloud just east of Yutu they called Yacana and they identified it as a llama. Yacana is the largest animal the Inca recognized in the Milky Way, and Yacana's two bright eyes stand out in the middle of the dark cloud. Yacana's two bright eyes are simply two bright stars—Alpha and Beta Centauri, two stars that together astronomers call Proxima Centauri, which is the closest star to earth. Take a look at the diagram of the dark cloud constellations that appears on the following Web site: *http://www.astronomy.pomona.edu/archeo/andes/startable3.html*.

In "Yacana the Llama and the Secret of Rain," the old man told the boy that he would see Yacana's eyes, and that she would lower her head to drink from the river. Because the Earth revolves around the Sun, the stars rise and set and so do the nebulae. The seasonal rise and set of the stars made Yacana appear to be ascending to the sky at one time of year and dipping her head into the river to drink at another time. Some myths say that when Yacana dips her head into the river she descends from the sky and drinks from the oceans on Earth to prevent the world from flooding. Some myths say that when she reaches the Earth she walks behind the rivers.

BELIEF: There is movement along the Milky Way.

When seen from Earth, the Milky Way does appear to move. It might look like flowing water, or because it's white, like flowing milk. But when the Inca watched the movement of the Milky Way and believed they saw flowing water and moving animals, they actually saw the rotation of our galaxy. Gravity makes the stars in the Milky Way tend to cluster together, and those clusters of stars revolve around the galaxy's nucleus. From space, the galaxy looks like a gigantic spinning disk. How much of the Milky Way we see depends on our location on Earth and on the season of the year.

BELIEF: The Milky Way could be used to track the seasons.

During planting season, farming people looked for signs that would help them know when to plant and when to reap and how to predict the fruitfulness of the harvest. The Inca looked at the dark cloud constellations to predict the rain. They watched the sky closely, so they noticed that when the dark cloud animals were obscured it meant rain, and when they were prominent it meant drought. The Inca saw changes on the Earth that corresponded to the movement of the heavens, so they used the dark cloud animals to time the seasons.

In "Yacana the Llama and the Secret of Rain," the dark cloud animals live in the celestial river, but because the Inca believed that the river originated on Earth, they believed that the dark cloud animals originated on Earth too. In fact, the Inca called these animals *Pachatira*, after Pachamama the Earth goddess. Both the Earth goddess and the dark cloud animals ensured fertility of the land. Some people said that the dark cloud animals entered the sky through the water when the Milky Way passed underground, and others said that they entered the sky from the mountains. Because the Inca considered the Milky Way a celestial river, they believed that it deposited water through the sky and that the water returned to the Earth as rain.

Machacuay winds himself around the constellation Scorpio, and in the Andes Mountains Machacuay and Scorpio rise right before it begins to rain. Machacuay looks like a giant snake that first shows his head in August and signals the time to plant, and then fills the sky in November and December when it rains the most. The Inca associated the snake with both the rainbow and the jagged streaks of lightning that accompanied rainstorms. Like the lightning, Machacuay disappeared when the rains stopped. Like the rainbow, he arched down to the horizon. Then he slipped into the river that passes underground. In the dry season, from May through July, Machacuay remains below the horizon, and he does not emerge again until the next time it begins to rain.

When people in the Northern Hemisphere first assigned images to the star-to-star constellations, they gave them forms of animals they connected with the season in which the stars appeared. They gave the stars of Leo the form of a lion for instance, because these appeared in the sky when the lion emerged from the desert during the summer drought. They gave the stars of Scorpio the form of a scorpion because these stars appeared when scorpions on Earth emerged from the ground.

The people in the Southern Hemisphere did this same thing when they assigned forms to the dark cloud constellations. Hanpatu the toad rose in the sky just as terrestrial toads came out of hibernation to mate, and Atoq the fox rose in the sky at summer solstice, the time when foxes on Earth give birth.

Once we understand the rotation of the Milky Way we can see the connection the ancient Peruvians saw between the dark clouds in the sky and the seasons of the Earth. And we can understand how the Peruvians gave the dark cloud animals credit for the fertility of the Earth and for the fertility of the animals. People always tried to find meaning in the movements of the sky. The Inca didn't know that the river was our galaxy and they didn't know that the animals they saw were simply dust and gas. But they did know that the river and the animals played a crucial role in the water cycle. The great river they saw spanning the heavens appeared to be a branch of their own river and a logical route for the water to flow from the sky to Earth. When the dark cloud constellations sunk below the horizon, the animals the Inca envisioned appeared to be dipping into the waters of Earth. When the dark cloud constellations rose above the horizon, the animals appeared to be carrying the water into the sky.

BELIEF: Watching the Milky Way can help us gain an understanding of the rhythms of the cosmos.

Once scientists learned that the Milky Way was a galaxy composed of stars and nebulae, it opened doors for understanding more and more about the structure and composition of the universe. Once scientists learned that many galaxies comprise the universe, they looked at other galaxies and studied the stars and nebulae within them and got glimpses of the universe in various stages of evolution. Galaxies have been called "island universes," and each one is a gigantic system powered by gravity. Gravity makes the stars in galaxies cluster together. By studying star clusters, astronomers see many stars that were born at roughly the same time.

The chapter on stars and constellations (Chapter 3) covers the birth and death of stars and explains how gravity created the star clusters that spin around the galaxy. Gravity also created the spiral structure of the galaxy. Billions of years ago when large clouds of gas were spinning slowly in space, they collapsed and became smaller, and, as they became smaller, they rotated faster and faster until those spinning dust clouds formed into spiral arms. The rotating star clusters revolve around the galaxy's nucleus, and scientists who study these clusters see stars in various stages of evolution. Studying the oldest stars gives scientists a glimpse into the early universe, and studying the nebulae helps them understand the earliest stages of star formation.

— TOPICS FOR DISCUSSION AND PROJECTS

TOPIC 1. Animals in the Sky

From antiquity people named the stars after animals whose seasonal cycles corresponded to the appearances or disappearances of certain stars. Early hunters of the ice age knew the seasonal migrations of animals, and they associated them with the seasonal behavior of the stars. In fact, this practice explains the existence of the zodiac, those twelve groups of stars that lie along the ecliptic and that people have connected with seasons of the year for centuries.

PROJECT IDEA

Have students identify some of the animals that the Inca saw in their world and find constellations in the southern sky that represent their celestial counterparts. Students can use the sky maps in *The Southern Sky Guide*, listed below, to identify constellations visible from the Southern Hemisphere and then draw dot-to-dot pictures of the animals the Inca likely recognized in the Milky Way.

SUGGESTED READING

Bierhorst, John. *Black Rainbow: Legends of the Incas and the Myths of Ancient Peru.* New York: Farrar, Straus and Giroux, 1976.

> Has myths featuring many of the animals in the Inca world.

Ellyard, David, and Wil Tirion. *The Southern Sky Guide.* New York: Cambridge University Press, 2001.

> Guide to the constellations of the southern sky, with maps and charts of the stars that appear each month. Includes legends of the southern constellations.

Kavanagh, James. *The Southern Night Sky.* Chandler, AZ: Waterford Press, 2001.

> Reference guide to the sky of the Southern Hemisphere. Has glow-in-the-dark star charts.

TOPIC 2. Inca Shrines and Ancient Observatories

In Inca culture *huacas* were defined as any material objects believed to have supernatural force. Huacas include many forms of natural phenomena such as mountains, trees, lakes, springs, caves, and rock and stone formations. These objects served as sacred shrines. They pockmark the Peruvian Andes and they likely served as both ceremonial centers and ancient observatories where the Inca watched celestial events that occurred on or near the horizon. In Cuzco, nearly 500 huacas lie along lines that radiate outward from a central temple like rays of the Sun. This system of landforms is called the *ceque system*, and the Coricancha is the Temple of the Sun. The Inca had originally covered the Coricancha in gold, but the Christian missionaries removed it in their attempt to banish the worship of false gods. The Inca believed that they descended from the Sun god Inti, and that the Milky Way ruled the Inca empire from the time of its birth to the time of its demise.

The temples these people built served as both places to honor the sky gods and places to observe the rhythms of the heavens. The Inca built one ceremonial site in the shape of a llama, and it contains both an unfinished astronomical observatory and a temple of the Sun. The elaborate myths the Inca told about the Sun and the Milky Way show that the Inca were astute observers of the sky.

PROJECT IDEA

Have students create a huaca that has connections to the Milky Way and that could serve as both a ceremonial center and an ancient observing place. Students might paint rocks and arrange them in the shape of one of the dark cloud animals, or they might create a diorama of a ceremonial site that includes an observatory decorated with celestial animals. Tell students to consider the river that stretches from the Earth to the sky and that dominates Inca myths. They might use that in their design also. The books below should give students an idea of what kinds of objects comprised the huacas of ancient Peru and how those objects helped define Inca myth and ritual.

SUGGESTED READING

Drew, David. *Inca Life*. Hauppauge, NY: Barron's Juveniles, 2000.

> Has much information on Inca architecture and artifacts. Geared toward children age ten and older.

Lourie, Peter. *Lost Treasure of the Inca*. Honesdale, PA: Boyds Mills Press, 1999.

> Aimed at children in grades 5–8. Contains information on arts and artifacts of the ancient Inca. Includes lots of color photographs.

Rees, Rosemary. *The Incas*. Chicago: Heinemann Library, 2002.

> Contains information on the Inca calendar, family life, and historical sites, artifacts, and art.

Scheff, Duncan. *Incas*. New York: Raintree Steck-Vaughn, 2001.

> Contains an overview of Inca history, culture, and archaeology.

Steele, Philip. *Inca World*. New York: Arness, 2000.

> Contains information on Inca life and culture and includes illustrations, maps, and class projects.

TOPIC 3. The River in the Sky

People in many parts of the world envisioned the Milky Way as a river, and "Yacana the Llama and the Secret of Rain" shows how the Inca populated their celestial river with the animals they recognized on Earth. Chinese myths that tell of the celestial Tien Ho, or the Silver River, show how the people from China envisioned tiny little fish swimming in this river and a great fish hook dangling above them, a hook that was really the crescent Moon. Myths of some lands say that the Milky Way serves as a path for dead souls to travel to the otherworld, and that the lights that sparkled along the path were campfires that lit the way.

PROJECT IDEA

Read other myths about the Milky Way in the source listed below. Then tell students to create their own myth based on the notion of the Milky Way as a river or path across the sky. Ask students to explain who might be traveling along that path and where they might be going.

SUGGESTED READING

Stryer, Andrea Sternn. *The Celestial River: Creation Tales of the Milky Way.* Little Rock, AR: August House Publishers, 1998.

> Contains a collection of legends from all over the world that give various interpretations of the Milky Way galaxy.

TOPIC 4. The Southern Sky

People who live north and south of the equator see different constellations. People in the Northern Hemisphere see constellations such as Orion and the Big Dipper, and people in the Southern Hemisphere see the Southern Cross and the dark cloud constellations that obscure the southern half of the Peruvian sky.

PROJECT IDEA

Use the readings below to obtain maps of the southern sky and the northern sky. Make photocopies of the maps and enlarge them. Then divide the class into two groups and create colorful star charts. Have students connect the dots and fill the charts with color pictures of some of the familiar constellations in each part of the sky.

SUGGESTED READING

Ellyard, David, and Wil Tirion. *The Southern Sky Guide*. New York: Cambridge University Press, 2001.

> Guide to the constellations of the southern sky, with maps and charts of the stars that appear each month. Includes legends of the southern constellations.

Kavanagh, James. *The Southern Night Sky*. Chandler, AZ: Waterford Press, 2001.

TOPIC 5.   Nebulae

The dark cloud constellations may only be clearly visible from the Southern Hemisphere, but people all over the world can see images in the clouds of dust and gas that float through the galaxy. When astronomers look through high-powered telescopes they recognize crabs, spiders, horses, and all kinds of images in these billowing clouds. This is similar to the way people recognize images in the atmospheric clouds that float through the summer sky. Most of these galactic clouds are only visible through telescopes, but scientists have been able to take pictures of these clouds and publish them for everyone to see.

PROJECT IDEA

Show students pictures of nebulae that appear in NASA's National Space Science Data Center image catalog and photo gallery (see Web address in Suggested Reading section below). Then tell students to choose one of the nebulae that particularly impresses them and paint a picture of the image they see when they look at the photograph. Have an art gallery in your classroom and display the students' paintings. Each student should prepare a note of explanation to post under their painting that includes scientific facts surrounding the nebula's formation, structure, and composition. The following list represents only a few of the numerous nebulae that might make beautiful paintings.

The Horsehead Nebula—This faint nebula lies in the constellation Orion just below Orion's belt. The Horsehead Nebula is one of the dark nebulae, and it was formed from two clouds rather than one.

The Tarantula Nebula—This nebula is not in the Milky Way but in a nearby galaxy called the Large Magellanic Cloud. The Tarantula Nebula is visible in the southern sky and it looks like a giant spider. It has also given birth to tens of thousands of stars—more stars than any other galaxy in the Local Group.

The Crab Nebula—This amazing structure is the remnant of a supernova explosion that occurred in 1054. It lies in the constellation Taurus and is fairly bright, though you still need a telescope to see it. The cloud looks like a giant crab, and inside it contains a small spinning star—a fragment of the original star that exploded centuries ago.

The Owl Nebula—This nebula lies just below the Big Dipper and it looks like the face of an owl. It's very old and it's one of the largest planetary nebulae in the galaxy.

The Ring Nebula—The Ring Nebula looks like a giant donut or a wedding band glowing in the constellation Lyra. It's a planetary nebula, one of 10,000 planetary nebulae in the sky.

Butterfly Nebula—The Butterfly Nebula is one of the many clouds of glowing gas that surround the bright star Deneb. The Butterfly Nebula and Deneb are in the distant constellation of Cygnus the swan.

Cat's Eye Nebula—The Cat's Eye Nebula is a planetary nebula that formed about 1,000 years ago. Scientists believe that when our Sun dies billions of years from now, it will undergo changes similar to those of the star that died and formed the Cat's Eye Nebula.

Lagoon Nebula—The Lagoon Nebula lies in the constellation Sagittarius, and it has a dark streak across the middle that looks like a lagoon.

The Rosette Nebula—The Rosette Nebula looks like a rose glowing in the constellation Monoceros.

The Eagle Nebula—The Eagle Nebula lies in the constellation Serpens and can sometimes be seen with binoculars.

SUGGESTED READING

Gallant, Roy. *Private Lives of the Stars*. New York: Macmillan, 1986.

Contains much information about star formation, star clusters, and nebulae, as well as information on stellar astronomy.

Mitton, Jacqueline. *Once Upon a Starry Night: A Book of Constellation Stories*. Washington, DC: National Geographic Society, 2003.

Contains facts and myths about nebulae, as well as stars, galaxies, and constellations.

NASA. "National Space Science Data Center." *http://nssdc.gsfc.nasa.gov*.

Has hundreds of images of nebulae, galaxies, the moon, the planets, comets, and asteroids.

Vogt, Gregory. *Nebulas*. New York: Raintree Steck-Vaughn, 2000.

Contains the science of different kinds of nebulae and how they're formed.

TOPIC 6. Galaxies Other than Our Own

The Milky Way belongs to a group of galaxies called the Local Group, which in addition to our own galaxy consists of about thirty galaxies. These galaxies include the Andromeda galaxy and the Large and Small Magellanic Clouds. The Andromeda galaxy is much larger than the Milky Way and has numerous smaller galaxies orbiting around it. The Magellanic Clouds are two irregular galaxies visible in the southern sky near the Milky Way. They feature prominently in myths told throughout the Southern Hemisphere, particularly in Polynesia where seafarers used them to aid in navigation and to predict the weather.

PROJECT IDEA

Have students choose a galaxy in the Local Group other than the Milky Way and describe some of its prominent features. Students can include well-known constellations and star clusters that lie within the galaxy, and they can include well-known nebulae and particularly bright stars.

SUGGESTED READING

Gustafson, John. *Stars, Clusters, and Galaxies*. Englewood Cliffs, NJ: Silver Burdett Press, 1993.

> Has lots of information on stars, clusters, galaxies, and nebulae, including activities and information on how to find them.

Kerrod, Robin. *Stars and Galaxies*. New York: Raintree Steck-Vaughn, 2002.

> Provides clear explanations, photos, diagrams, and a helpful list of Web sites.

Sipiera, Paul B. *Galaxies*. New York: Children's Press, 1997.

Vogt, Gregory. *The Milky Way and Other Galaxies*. New York: Raintree Steck-Vaughn, 2000.

> Contains a scientific exploration of the Milky Way and other galaxies in the universe.

—— SUGGESTED READING FOR TEACHERS

Aveni, Anthony. *Stairways to the Stars: Skywatching in Three Great Ancient Cultures.* New York: John Wiley, 1999.

> An excellent overview of astronomy and calendrics in the civilizations of the Maya and the Inca, and on the builders of Stonehenge. The chapter on the Inca covers astronomical symbolism of the Coricancha in Cuzco, and an explanation of the ceque system.

Bauer, Brian S., and David S. Dearborn. *Astronomy and Empire in the Ancient Andes: The Cultural Origins of Inca Skywatching.* Austin: University of Texas Press, 1995.

> Offers lots of information on Inca astronomy, including beliefs about the Milky Way and the dark cloud constellations.

Bierhorst, John. *Black Rainbow: Legends of the Incas and the Myths of Ancient Peru.* New York: Farrar, Straus and Giroux, 1976.

> Has myths featuring many of the animals in the Inca world.

Cobo, Father Bernabé. *Inca Religion and Customs.* Translated and edited by Roland Hamilton. Austin: University of Texas Press, 1990.

> Classic work on the Inca, including information on Inca astronomy and beliefs about the Milky Way.

Krupp, E. C. *Beyond the Blue Horizon: Myths and Legends of the Sun, Moon, Stars, and Planets.* New York: Oxford University Press, 1991.

> A chapter entitled "Along the Milky Way" discusses the dark cloud constellations and the Inca view of the Milky Way galaxy.

Sesti, Guiseppe Maria. *The Glorious Constellations: History and Mythology.* New York: Abrams, 1991.

> Discusses the myths of the Milky Way. Beautiful illustrations.

Sullivan, William. *The Secret of the Incas: Myth, Astronomy, and the War Against Time.* New York: Crown, 1999.

> Contains information on Inca astronomy and includes a detailed explanation of myths and beliefs surrounding the Milky Way and the dark cloud constellations.

Urton, Gary. *At the Crossroads of Earth and Sky.* Austin: University of Texas Press, 1988.

> A detailed overview of Inca astronomy, including information on the science, myth, and observation of the dark cloud constellations.

———. *Inca Myths.* Austin: University of Texas Press, 1999.

> Provides an explanation of the myths of the Inca, including those of the sky.

6 .... Comets

THE MYTHS OF COMETS

Comets have surfaced in myths and legends as evil omens. They appeared in the sky to herald the occurrence of natural disasters such as floods and famines. They served as warnings of impending war and the death of powerful rulers.

The appearance of a comet in 44 B.C. was interpreted differently than other comets in history, particularly because it lit the sky over Rome just after the death of Julius Caesar. Some of the Roman philosophers saw disaster in the comet. They connected it to the riots and chaos that threatened to destroy the city after the emperor's death, and they connected it to the great civil war that broke out between Augustus and Antony over the leadership of Rome. Augustus, then known as Octavius, was Caesar's adopted son, and he saw this comet as a perfect opportunity to ensure that he succeed Caesar as leader. Augustus convinced the people that the comet was the soul of Caesar ascending to heaven. Most everyone in Rome believed him.

Read the following story and discover how Augustus gained the leadership of Rome. Then discuss how the story reflects early superstitions about comets as fiery messengers of the gods.

"Caesar's Comet," a Myth from Rome

In 44 B.C., on the Ides of March, death touched the lives of all the people of Rome. Julius Caesar, their ruler, was dead. There had been a conspiracy, plotted by powerful men who wished to end Caesar's rule, and the Ides of March was slated as his death day all along. Now the Roman dictator lay murdered in the streets. Chaos broke out in the land.

Caesar had been warned about the Ides of March, for omens and prophecies in those days took many forms and came from people who had connections with the sky powers. It was a soothsayer who warned Caesar of this day, and the powerful ruler of Rome listened but took no heed. But messages from the gods could not be overlooked, nor could omens of doom or indications of divine intervention be disregarded. Sometimes omens and prophecies appeared in the heavens, as if the gods themselves were sending messages from the sky.

Julius Caesar had served as the leader of Rome in a time when people looked to the heavens for guidance and paid homage to Venus and Apollo and all the gods and goddesses who lived in the sky and set the laws of the land. The temple of Venus stood in the Forum, erected by Caesar to honor the goddess as his divine ancestor. Julius Caesar claimed himself as a descendent of Venus, which made him a divine king and gave him a godly right to rule.

Julius Caesar was indeed a powerful ruler and he amassed a large number of supporters who upheld his right to dictate the law. But most rulers as powerful as Caesar also had enemies, and Caesar had some powerfully violent ones. Cassius was Caesar's greatest enemy. He believed that Caesar had too much power and that his dictatorship threatened the state of Rome. So Cassius plotted to gain the favor of Brutus, one of the most respected citizens of Rome, and to convince Brutus that Caesar must be halted in order to save the country. Brutus had always been loyal to Caesar, so convincing him to oppose his leader was no small task. But Cassius succeeded in convincing him, and the two of them plotted to kill Caesar on the Ides of March.

Caesar had been warned, but he paid no attention to the soothsayer. On the 15th day of March, Caesar lay dead in the streets. Brutus tried to convince the public that Caesar had to die to save Rome. He told them that it was dangerous for Caesar to have too much power. But Marc Antony tried to convince the public otherwise. Marc Antony was a great general in the Roman army and one of Caesar's greatest supporters, and he himself had plans to take over as ruler of Rome. But after Caesar's murder fighting broke out in the streets. The Romans who supported Brutus and Cassius and the Romans who supported Marc Antony fought bloody battles. Chaos led to civil war, and Rome had no leader.

There were plenty of people who wanted to be leader, and for quite some time the power of Rome was divided among three of Caesar's generals: Marc Antony, Lepidus, and Octavius, Caesar's nephew. Each of them wanted to assume the crown and carry on the leadership of Caesar alone. Quarrels among them prevented them from ruling effectively together. Then Marc Antony, the most competent of the three generals, traveled to Egypt and fell madly in love with Cleopatra, the Queen of Egypt, and neglected his duties in Rome. Rome was in trouble. Pompeius, a leader who opposed Caesar, threatened to seize Rome and wrest the rule from its new leaders. With Antony out of the country, he had every bit of confidence that he could do so.

Marc Antony was in love, but he answered the call of his country and tore himself away from Cleopatra. Lepidus bailed, and Antony and Octavius together defeated Pompeius and carried Rome. But eventually Marc Antony returned to Egypt, and to Cleopatra, which caused a rift with Octavius. A battle ensued between the two men. Marc Antony left Cleopatra to fight, and she rebelled against him and joined forces with Octavius.

Now the love between Antony and Cleopatra is a story for another day, and a tragic story at that. But when Cupid, the god of love, imposes his will on human beings, it has profound effects, and it affected the fate of Rome as surely as did the comet that lit the skies. Octavius won the battle with Antony, and at eighteen years of age, he became leader of the world. He declared himself Caesar Augustus, and the Roman Empire was born.

There were many indications that something miraculous would happen to Rome, and there were many people in those times who learned how to interpret the signs from the heavens. The soothsayer knew to warn Caesar to beware the Ides of March, and the gods that sent the soothsayer this message sent messages in other ways too, by stirring nature to action in demonstrations of godly force. Mt. Etna, a volcano in Sicily, erupted in the spring, close to the time of Caesar's death, and it filled the air over Rome with a haze of volcanic ash. Some said that the giant Enceladous was imprisoned under Mt. Etna and was tugging at his chains, and others said that Vulcan, the fire god, was forging his weapons in his smith shop under the Earth. For whatever reason the volcano erupted, the gods had sent a message. And the people of Rome interpreted it as a sign of impending doom.

The gods had another message for the people, however, and they chose Venus to deliver it. The goddess sat enthroned in her temple while the Romans played games in the street and held festivities all around her. Octavius, then known as Augustus, instigated games at the temple, and he held the games at the festival in honor of his father, who had established the festival years before. Then, as everyone celebrated, a bright light flashed through the heavens. The people looked up in awe and fright. Augustus recognized an opportunity when he saw one. He addressed the people and declared the comet a sign of Caesar's godhood. Venus had emerged from the temple to carry Caesar to heaven and to light the sky to announce his arrival to the world.

"Caesar has joined the rank of the gods," Augustus told the people.

Augustus, as Caesar's son, inherited the divine right to rule.

"It is Caesar, our king!" someone cried from the crowd. "He has risen to godhood!"

"The soul of our king is soaring to heaven!" cried someone else.

"Hail Caesar," one of the men cried, and the countrymen rejoiced. "Hail Caesar!" everyone shouted. "Our king has returned and he is divine! Hail Caesar, the god-king! Ruler of all Rome! Hail Augustus, our leader, son of the divine!"

The comet shone brightly for seven days and convinced the Romans that Caesar had risen to heaven and achieved the status of a god. They believed that Venus, their goddess, had carried his soul to the sky, and that Augustus, Caesar's son, should assume the position as godhead. Caesar's rule was divine, his power absolute, and the comet had blazed forth to ensure it. Seven days later, Rome had its first emperor, Augustus had secured his divine rule, and the comet disappeared from the sky.

....

"Caesar's Comet" was created from plot summaries of Shakespeare's *Julius Caesar* and *Antony and Cleopatra* and from miscellaneous accounts of the comet related in early Roman philosophical texts and from information presented in *The Comet of 44 B.C. and Caesar's Funeral Games* (Atlanta, GA: Scholars Press, 1997), by John T. Ramsey and A. Lewis Licht.

THE SCIENCE OF COMETS

Our understanding of comets has come a long way from the days when people could believe that a bright light flashing across the sky had supernatural power. But for a long time people did assign comets such power, and in most cases they feared comets as omens of doom. Because of the reputation comets had as agents of some strange supernatural force, Augustus used the comet of 44 B.C. to his own political advantage. He used it to elevate Julius Caesar to godhood and to ensure his own right to rule based on his position as the son of a god.

....

BELIEF: Comets are strange and chaotic intruders.

There's nothing unusual or chaotic about comets; they're an ordinary part of our solar system and they're simply made of ice and dust. Comets orbit the Sun like the planets do, but they have highly elliptical orbits that carry them very close to the Sun and very far out into the solar system. No one knows exactly how many comets are out there or how big they are, but there are billions of them in the far reaches of space. They're invisible when they're far out in the solar system, but they flash over the Earth when they get close to the Sun.

Comets are not particularly strange but they are eccentric, in part because their orbits vary drastically. Long-period comets can take thousands of years to orbit the Sun but short-period comets, like Halley's Comet, orbit the Sun in 200 years or less. We don't always see these comets, but they're there. They come close to the Sun and the Earth, but many are simply not bright enough for observers to see without powerful telescopes. Though the orbits of comets do ensure that they regularly visit the Earth, we can't always rely on comets to visit the Earth exactly on schedule. Halley's Comet for instance, has an orbital period of seventy-six years, but the gravitational pull of the planets alters its orbit. This means that Halley's Comet, though reliable, can actually appear three or so years late. Long before scientists learned to calculate comets' orbits, comets appeared to show up unexpectedly and for no reason. So people searched for a reason. In ancient Rome, Caesar Augustus gave them one.

Once Caesar Augustus explained that the comet indicated Caesar's arrival in heaven, the people no longer feared that chaos was descending on the world. Before they accepted Augustus's explanation they saw death and destruction ravage the Earth, and they watched an eerie haze blanket the sky. Of course, death and destruction often occur when a country is in turmoil, and it appears that the haze in the sky simply came from Mt. Etna, a volcano in Sicily, just south of Rome. Mt. Etna had erupted just months before the appearance of Caesar's comet, and at the time of the games, the smoke and ash from the eruption still lingered in the sky. Because in Roman times, volcanoes indicated shows of godly power and examples of chaos in the universe, the eruption of Mt. Etna close to Caesar's death magnified the significance of the event—and the significance of the comet.

FIGURE 6.1 · The Orbit of Halley's Comet

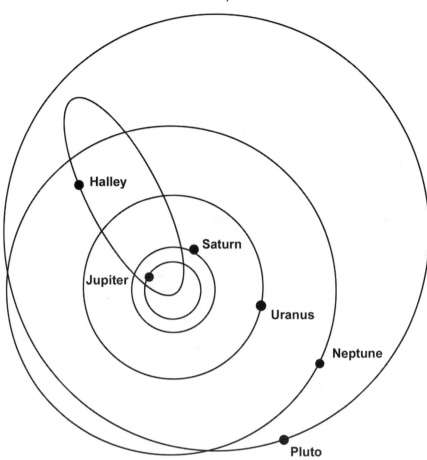

BELIEF: Comets appear mysteriously out of nowhere.

Comets don't simply materialize out of nowhere; they reside in the so-lar system and spend most of their time in certain areas of the solar system far away from the Sun. Most long-period comets come from an area of the solar system called the Oort Cloud, which exists far beyond the planet Pluto. Most short-period comets come from an area of the solar system called the Kuiper Belt, a region closer in, but still beyond the planet Neptune. The Oort Cloud and the Kuiper Belt are believed to be disk-shaped areas that completely surround the planets' orbits. Because comets spend most of their time in these areas, they rarely appear over the Earth. They remain out in the dark, cold regions of space where they exist as frozen balls of dust and ice that scientists often call "dirty snowballs." Look at the orbit of Halley's Comet shown in Figure 6.1. You can see that while the orbits of planets are close to round, the orbits of comets are elliptical. This explains why comets come much closer to the Sun at certain times than at others, and it explains why they take such a long time to appear over the Earth.

When a comet flashed through the sky after Caesar's death it had a tremendous impact, not only on the scientific record but also on the future of Rome. The comet was bright enough to light the skies in the daytime, and it shone for seven days in a row in the month of July, just as the people of Rome were participating in games instigated in honor of their murdered dictator. Daytime comets are extremely rare; usually they're only visible at sunrise and sunset. In this case, the smoke in the air made the comet seem exceptionally bright. Of course neither the brightness of this comet nor the length of time it appeared in the sky had anything to do with Julius Caesar. Strange as it might have seemed at the time, bright conspicuous comets might be visible to observers on Earth about once every decade. Though comets bright enough to see with the naked eye actually flash above the Earth about once a year, astronomers looking through large telescopes might see two or three dozen comets on any clear night.

BELIEF: Comets are fiery visitors from the sky.

When comets exist in the Oort Cloud or the Kuiper Belt or whenever their orbits take them far away from the Sun, there's nothing fiery about them. In fact, they only shine when the Sun's light reflects off of them. When a comet moves into the inner solar system however, and when it gets close to the Sun, its surface heats up. The ice vaporizes and turns to gas, and that gas forms a cloud around the comet's nucleus that can span hundreds of thousands of miles. This cloud of gas is called the *coma*, and the coma makes the comet appear fuzzy to observers on Earth. As the comet gets closer to the Sun it grows larger and brighter. The brightness of a comet depends on the brightness of the coma, and the brightness of the coma depends on the size and composition of the nucleus. It also depends on how close the comet gets to the Sun and how close it gets to the Earth. A comet is usually the brightest near *perihelion*, which is the point of its orbit that is closest to the Sun.

Look at Figure 6.2. This diagram shows the parts of a comet. All comets have a nucleus, a coma, and a tail. They have only a nucleus when they're in the outer reaches of the solar system, and they acquire the coma and tail when they move toward the Sun. When the comet gets very close to the Sun, solar radiation and a steady flow of charged particles push material from the coma away from the Sun and form a long, glowing tail.

FIGURE 6.2 · The Parts of a Comet

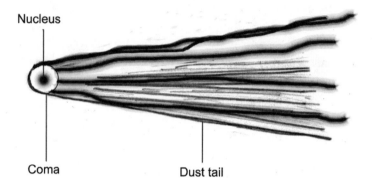

Solar particles continually blow off the Sun's surface, and when they collide with material from the comet they blow it backward. The word comet comes from the Greek term *kometes*, which means "long haired." "Long-haired" refers to the comet's tail. The tail of the comet is always opposite the Sun. The debris that blows off the Sun is called *solar wind*, and solar wind affects the comet much like typical wind effects a flag. When wind hits a flag, the flag's fabric blows outward in the opposite direction, and when solar wind hits a comet, the comet's tail blows outward and away from the Sun. A comet's orbit determines its proximity to the Sun and the Earth. A comet's proximity to the Sun and the Earth determines its behavior and appearance. The closer a comet gets to the Sun, the hotter and brighter it becomes, and the closer a comet gets to the Earth, the brighter it appears to us.

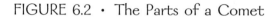

BELIEF: Comets are messages from the sky gods.

Take a look at Table 6.1, which lists the dates of upcoming comets. People have recorded the appearance of comets since prehistory. Records

TABLE 6.1 · Upcoming Comets

Comet	Constellation	Date
Tempel 1	Virgo	June, 2005
Chernykh	Vetus	October, 2005
Schwassmann-Wachmann 3	Hercules	May, 2006
Honda-Mrkos Pajdusakova	Aries	June, 2006
Faye	Pisces	November, 2006

of Halley's Comet date back to 240 B.C. They existed in ancient Babylon and China, and even in ice records in the glaciers of Greenland. Halley's Comet is probably the best-known comet of the thousands that exist in our solar system, and it has made regular appearances over the Earth roughly once every seventy-six years. Halley's Comet last appeared over the Earth in 1986 and we expect it to appear again in 2061. But in the ancient world the common people had no idea about the cycles of comets. These mysterious intruders flashed across an ordered sky like fiery demons from another world, or like messages from powerful sky gods.

Once scientists understood the composition and behavior of comets, they no longer considered them fiery messages. But scientists believe that comets formed five billion years ago when the Sun and the planets of the solar system formed, so in some sense comets do serve as messages. Comets serve as messages from an ancient world. Because they remain frozen much of the time, they tell us about the age and composition of the early solar system. Comets also help astronomers understand the science of solar wind and solar energy and about the magnetic fields of the planets.

BELIEF: The appearance of comets coincides with earthly events, such as the birth or death of powerful rulers.

Strange as it may seem, the appearance of comets often did coincide with the birth and death of powerful rulers. This has happened time and again throughout history, as recently as 1997 when the comet Hale-Bopp flashed through the skies the same year Princess Diana died. Given the significance early people assigned to shows of nature's force, it makes sense that people drew connections between the bright lights that flashed through their sky and the birth and death of kings. In the sixteenth century William Shakespeare acknowledged this ancient belief in eloquent words:

> When beggars die there are no comets seen;
> The heavens themselves blaze forth the death of princes.

* * * * * * * * * * * * * * * * * * * *

Julius Caesar, III.ii.31–32

These lines show how people connected celestial occurrences with earthly events. They show how the people of Rome assigned significance to comets and specifically how they connected the comet of 44 B.C. to the death of Julius Caesar. Scientifically speaking however, comets travel in orbits and are simply part of nature's rhythm. They're eccentric but they do follow a pattern. Years of studying comets has helped scientists understand why they act in strange ways.

We have already learned that the orbits of comets vary greatly, and that the gravitational forces from the planets often alter those orbits. Sometimes the gravitational forces of the planets can alter the orbits of comets drastically by pulling long-period comets out of their paths and into shorter orbits. That's what happened to Halley's Comet and to another famous comet called Swift-Tuttle. Halley's Comet and Swift-Tuttle are now short-period comets, but many scientists believe that they once followed much larger and much more elliptical orbits until encounters with planets, particularly Jupiter, shortened their orbits by swinging them closer to the Sun. When gravity pulls comets out of orbit, they can spin out of the solar system completely or collide with the planet and destruct on impact. When these collisions occur, they cause impact craters. We know that the Moon has numerous impact craters, but for every crater on the moon, the Earth once had twenty more.

BELIEF: Comets are omens of doom.

In "Caesar's Comet," before Augustus explained the significance of the comet's appearance the citizens of Rome feared the flash of light in their skies as an omen of death, destruction, and political unrest. This was a typical reaction in ancient times. But even though comets are scientific phenomena and not omens delivered by supernatural means, scientists now recognize a scientific reason to fear comets. They can impact the Earth. Because they orbit the Sun, like the Earth and the planets, they can collide with the Earth and the planets. And they do—more often than people realize.

The chances are only about one in 10,000 that a comet large enough to cause global catastrophe will hit the Earth in our lifetime, though tons of debris smaller than grains of sand enter the Earth's atmosphere and burn up everyday. Some of the larger debris does land on Earth as meteorites. When the debris burns up in the Earth's atmosphere, we see meteors or "shooting stars."

Comets, asteroids, and meteoroids are all rocks from space, but they differ from each other in several respects. Asteroids originate in the inner solar system in the asteroid belt, an area between the orbits of Jupiter and Saturn. Asteroids are made of rock or metal. Comets originate in the outer solar system, in the Oort Cloud or the Kuiper Belt, and they're made of rock and ice. Meteoroids originate from comets or asteroids, and they form when asteroids collide or when comets pass near the Sun and the solar heat releases dust from the comet's tail. Though large space rocks impact the Earth only once every hundred million years or so, about eighty small ones collide with the Earth about once a week. Most of them explode over the ocean or in remote areas of the land, far away from civilization, and no one even knows what happened. Most of these rocks hit the Earth's atmosphere but break up before they fall, so what debris does make it to the ground causes no impact at all. That's what happened in 1908 when a giant space rock hit the Earth near the Tungusta River in a remote part of Siberia. The rock broke up in the air before it hit the ground so it left no impact. But it set millions of trees on fire. In 1994 the Comet Shoemaker-Levy slammed into the planet Jupiter. It also broke up before it hit the ground.

Today most scientists agree that an impact from a comet killed the dinosaurs. Once scientists recognized that, they began to work on calculating when impacts could affect the Earth and they began devising ways to protect the Earth from destruction. Scientists in the United States, France, Canada, and China currently search for any object in space that might be on a collision course with Earth and they plan the best way to break up the object before an impact can occur. Given the fact that comets and asteroids continue to collide with the Earth every day, it's fortunate that science has taught us a way to fight the threat of cometary impacts. Today, detecting comets has become a fascinating area of research.

— TOPICS FOR DISCUSSION AND PROJECTS

TOPIC 1. The Notion of Divine Kingship

When Augustus assumed the power of Rome, the Roman Empire was born, and this happened largely because of Caesar's comet. So Caesar's comet became known as the *sidus Iulium* ("Julian star"), and it became a symbol of the new age. Once Augustus announced the significance of the comet and once people accepted his explanation and made him emperor, a bright star was added to Caesar's head on a statue of the late ruler. Augustus placed a star on his own head as well, on his helmet, to indicate his connection to Caesar and his godly right to rule the land. He then took the bronze statue of Caesar, with the star on its head, to the temple of Venus, and a bright star became an emblem of the late king.

PROJECT IDEA

Have students design a hat, like the helmet Augustus wore, or have them design another article of clothing or military weapon that might have been used by a Roman emperor. They should decorate their hats or weapons or articles of clothing with astronomical symbols that indicate power and godhood.

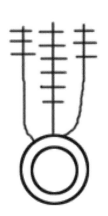 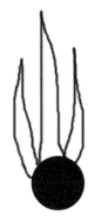

SUGGESTED READING

Houston, Mary G. *Ancient Greek, Roman, and Byzantine Costume*. Mineola, NY: Dover Publications, 2003.

Contains facts and illustrations of costumes from Rome.

Picken, Mary Brooks. *A Dictionary of Costume and Fashion: Historical and Modern*. Mineola, NY: Dover, 1999.

Includes 750 illustrations as well as definitions of costume terms.

Steele, Philip. *Clothing and Crafts in Roman Times*. Milwaukee, WI: Gareth Stevens, Inc., 2000.

Contains information and illustrations of Roman clothing, jewelry, metalwork, and masks. Includes craft projects.

Warry, John Gibson. *Greece and Rome at War*. Norman: University of Oklahoma Press, 1995.

Appropriate for both kids and adults, this book has informative text as well as color drawings of Roman uniforms, equipment, and weapons.

TOPIC 2. Astronomical Objects as Symbols of Power

The silver coins used in ancient Rome were called Denarii, and the Denarii of Augustus's time serve as an example of just how the Roman government used comets for political propaganda. The Romans wanted the people to believe that Caesar was a powerful god, so they inscribed the ancient silver coins with words that mean "divine Julius."

The comet of 44 B.C. was not the only astronomical event the Romans used as political propaganda; and the coins depicting images of Caesar's comet were not the only coins to display astronomical objects as symbols of power. Other Roman coins show images of a solar eclipse, for instance, because the Romans declared the solar eclipse that occurred on November 11 in 120 B.C. as divine support for their success in conquering southern France.

PROJECT IDEA

Have students design a collection of coins that use astronomical objects as symbols of power. They can use white cardboard or poster board to create round coins and then decorate the coins with various images.

SUGGESTED READING

Buggey, T. J. "Astronomical Symbols on Ancient Coins." On-line at: *http://www.people.memphis.edu/~tjbuggey.astro.html*.

LaPrevotte, Diane. "Ancient Treasure Coins." *http://www.ancient-treasure.com*.

 Contains links to info on ancient coins and their symbolism.

Sayles, Wayne G. *Ancient Coin Collecting*. Iola, WI: Krause Publications, 2003.

 Contains over 200 photographs as well as information on collecting.

Van Meter, David. *Handbook of Roman Imperial Coins*. New York: Sanford J. Durst, 2000.

 Contains photographs and information about the coins of the Roman Empire.

TOPIC 3. The Roman Festival and the Games

Caesar made himself popular with the people by staging an annual festival and putting on elaborate shows for public spectators. The festival included horseracing, musical contests, and staged battles between military soldiers and exotic animals. When Augustus gained the leadership of Rome, he continued Caesar's festival and added games to the event that he dedicated to Venus and held in Caesar's honor. It was during these public games that the comet appeared.

PROJECT IDEA

Read about the Roman festival and the games, and make a classroom mural depicting the various games and activities. Or stage a class play of "Caesar's Comet." Use the Roman festival as the setting and show the actors participating in some of the games the people played long ago. Be sure to incorporate the comet into the scenery and into the script. Include the statue. Decorate Augustus's helmet with a star.

SUGGESTED READING

Bentley, Nancy, and Donna Guthrie. *Putting on a Play: The Young Playwright's Guide to Scripting, Directing, and Performing.* Brookfield, CT: Millbrook Press, 1996.

> A step-by-step guide that focuses on scriptwriting but also includes instructions for producing plays.

Korty, Carol. *Writing Your Own Plays: Creative Adapting and Improvising.* Studio City, CA: Players Press, 2000.

> Helps students and teachers create plays and guides them through the process from scripting to production.

Nardo, Don. *The Games of Ancient Rome.* San Diego, CA: Lucent Books, 2000.

> Explains the origins of the Roman public games and relates them to politics and government. Discusses the life of the gladiators and explains the chariot races and other games. Includes photographs, maps, and a glossary.

Olivova, Vera. *Sports and Games in the Ancient World.* New York: St. Martin's Press, 1985.

> Covers the origin and atmosphere of the public games of Greece and Rome and the origin of the Olympics. Includes related art.

Superstitions still exist today that have their base in early beliefs about scientific phenomena. Superstition was rampant in early Rome, which was why the people so readily believed Augustus when he explained the comet as the soul of Caesar.

PROJECT IDEA

Divide students into groups and have them prepare reports on superstitions to present to the class. The books below will help students identify superstitions that relate to numerous areas of science, including astronomy, as well as to everyday life.

SUGGESTED READING

Delys, Claudia, ed. *A Treasury of Superstitions*. New York: Random House, 1997.

> A dictionary of superstitions in culture, science, and everyday life.

Ruchlis, Hy. *How Do You Know It's True? Discovering the Difference Between Science and Superstition*. Amherst, NY: Prometheus, 1991.

> Contains interesting facts and superstitions including many that relate to astronomy and astrology. Written for young adults.

Schwartz, Alvin. *Cross Your Fingers, Spit in Your Hat: Superstitions and Other Beliefs*. New York: HarperTrophy, 1993.

> Contains a collection of superstitions that have molded belief throughout history.

TOPIC 5. Shakespeare's Caesar

William Shakespeare's famous tragedy *Julius Caesar* was one of the longest-running plays performed at the Globe Theatre in London and it has since been continually performed and adapted. By familiarizing themselves with the play and discussing Caesar's influence and the events surrounding his rule and his death, students will gain not only a better understanding of one of the world's most influential historical figures and one of the world's most influential playwrights, but also a better understanding how the people of Rome so readily accepted the comet of 44 B.C. as Caesar's ghost.

PROJECT IDEA

Treat students to Shakespeare's play *Julius Caesar* either by assigning students parts and reading the play aloud in class or by listening to a recording of the play in class.

SUGGESTED READING

Davidson, Diane. *Julius Caesar for Young People*. New Hyde Park, NY: Learning Links, Inc. 1990.

> An abridged version of the original text with summaries of parts deleted, for grades 5–8.

Shakespeare, William. *Julius Caesar*. Mineola, NY: Dover, 1993.

> An audiocassette that condenses the play to just over an hour.

———. *Julius Caesar*. Edited by Alan Durband. Hauppauge, NY: Barron's Educational Series, 1985.

> An adaptation of Shakespeare's classic geared toward grades 5–8. Available in both book and audio format.

———. *Julius Caesar*. Read by LA Theatre Works staff. New York: Random House Audio Publishing Group, 1998.

> This retelling of Shakespeare's classic includes references to Caesar's comet.

TOPIC 6. Famous Comets

When Caesar's Comet appeared in the sky in 44 B.C., it created quite a stir with the Roman people. When Comet Hale-Bopp appeared in the sky in 1997, it made a big splash with astronomers. Comet Hale-Bopp is one of the most famous comets in history, but there are others that are equally famous. Each of the comets listed below has made an appearance over Earth in the last ten years and achieved status as a famous visitor from the outer solar system.

PROJECT IDEA

Have students choose one of the famous comets listed below and create a poster and a report to present to the class. They can include information about the comet's discovery and report on what scientists have learned about it. Have them draw a diagram of the comet's orbit and include any other information that might help explain what makes this comet unique.

> **Comet Halley**—The most famous comet in history.
>
> **Comet Hale-Bopp**—Made its last appearance over Earth in 1997 and won't return again for 2,500 years.
>
> **Comet Hyakutake**—Made its last appearance in 1996 and won't return again for 40,000 years. In 1996 it had the largest tail ever recorded.
>
> **Comet Shoemaker-Levy 9**—Made big news in 1994 when it smashed into the planet Jupiter.
>
> **Comet Tempel-Tuttle**—Made its last appearance in February, 1998, and returns every thirty-three years in November. When it returns, it causes the most spectacular meteor showers!

SUGGESTED READING

Dahlquist, Teresa, and Raf Dahlquist. *Mister Halley and His Comet*. Canoga Park, CA: Polestar Nexus, 1986.

NASA Jet Propulsion Laboratory. "Stardust Education Site." *http://stardust.jpl.nasa.gov/classroom*.

> Has activities for researching famous comets. Geared toward grades 5–8.

Sky & Telescope Radio Series. "Sky Online." *http://skyandtelescope.com*.

—— SUGGESTED READING FOR TEACHERS

Burnham, R. *Great Comets*. England: Cambridge University Press, 2001.

> Discusses the significance of the great comets to the study of astronomy and culture, and covers the myth and history surrounding appearances of great comets of the past.

Crovisier, J., and T. Encrenaz, *Comet Science—The Study of Remnants from the Birth of the Solar System*. England: Cambridge University Press, 2000.

> Contains a comprehensive overview of historical beliefs surrounding comets and a thorough discussion of current research and the significance of studying comets to understand the solar system. Gives special attention to the famous comets Hyakutake and Hale-Bopp. Illustrated.

Frazer, James George. *The Illustrated Golden Bough*. New York: Doubleday, 1978.

> Classic work that contains much information about superstition that inspired myths and ritual relating to natural phenomena.

Ramsey, John T., and Lewis Licht. *The Comet of 44 B.C. and Caesar's Funeral Games*. Atlanta, GA: Scholars Press, 1997.

> Includes recent research on the identification and significance of the great comet that impacted the history of Rome.

Sagan, Carl, and A. Druyan. *Comet*. New York: Random House, 1990.

> Explores comets in myth, legend, and research.

Schaaf, F. *A Comet of the Century—from Halley to Hale-Bopp*. New York: Copernicus, 1997.

> Contains an introduction to comets that includes detailed information on the great comets as well as theories of comets that have emerged in myth and culture.

Schechner, Sara. *Comets, Popular Culture and the Birth of Modern Cosmology*. Princeton, NJ: Princeton University Press, 1999.

> Contains an overview of comets in culture and in science, with much information on the myths, legends, and superstitions surrounding comets.

Sumners, Carolyn, and Carlton Allen. *Cosmic Pinball*. New York: McGraw-Hill, 1999.

> Includes information on famous comets and meteor showers, and covers the myths and history of comets as well as the latest research.

Yeomans, D. *Comets—A Chronological History of Observation, Science, Myth, and Folklore*. New York: John Wiley, 1991.

> Provides a historical overview of comets in myth and science.

7 .... Meteors

THE MYTHS OF METEORS

Before scientists understood meteors, ancient people came up with stories of their own to explain their existence. Many people connected meteors to the weather, and many people connected them to fire. Some people connected meteors to the Moon, and others connected them to the stars. Every culture that witnessed meteors found them spectacular, but most everyone also found them frightening. These were people who looked to the sky for order and were comforted to see the celestial bodies move in predictable patterns. When something strange and mysterious appeared in the sky it indicated chaos in the universe, and when flaming streaks of light shot down from heaven to Earth, it seemed as if the stars were falling from the sky.

Because early people feared meteors, many meteor myths emphasized their association with evil and death. Early skywatchers paid close attention to events they witnessed in the heavens, and they knew the stars were supposed to stay in the sky. If the stars fell from the sky, people figured that it must be a bad omen or a warning from an angry sky god. If the stars fell from the sky, some people feared that the world would end.

The following myth was told by the Skidi Pawnee Indians of the Central Plains to explain the mysterious objects that fell from the sky and appeared to be gifts from the sky gods. Though meteors have been recorded in legend all over the world, North America has a rich body of meteor myths, and the Pawnee have a particularly rich body of star-lore. Read the myth below and discuss how it reflects early beliefs about meteors and meteorites. Then use The Science of Meteors section to explain the facts about meteors. A list of topics for discussion and projects follows.

"METEOR'S CHILD," A MYTH FROM NORTH AMERICA

Long before white men came to America, and long before city lights flooded the central Plains, the Pawnee huddled by fires outside their earth lodges and watched the sky. The night was dark and clear and the gods in the heavens watched over the Pawnee and lit their world with the power of starlight. The Pawnee worshipped the sky, and they prayed to the star gods who guided and protected them. Tirawahat, the great god, ruled the heavens. It was through Tirawahat's power that the Pawnee lived on Earth, and it was through Tirawahat's goodness that Pahokatawa, Meteor's child, came to the people.

The stars that lit the Pawnee world carried powers that brought life to all in existence. The people had many stories about the stars and about the way they moved through the heavens and ordered the world. But sometimes the stars fell through the sky. This frightened people. The Pawnee lived by the rules set forth by the regular movements of heaven's nightlights. When the stars flashed streaks of light through the darkness and shot downward toward Earth, the people huddled outside their earth lodges and feared that the world would end.

Tirawahat, the great sky god, made sure that the world would not end. He sent a star to Earth to guide and protect the Pawnee people. On a dark night, across a dark sky, this bright star fell from the heavens and landed on the plains. By the grace of Tirawahat, Pahokatawa, the great Skidi warrior, had returned to the village. From that day forward, he protected the people from death and disease, just as he had when he lived among them long ago.

It was long before this star fell to Earth when Pahokatawa lived among the people and bravely fought battles against enemy tribes. It was so long before the star fell that when Pahokatawa returned no one knew him, for he lived among the Pawnee people long before any of the new generation were born. These people knew of Pahokatawa's existence however, because stories of his bravery had passed through the village from generation to generation. The elders told stories about Pahokatawa in their earth lodges and around their fires to keep their great warrior's memory alive. They told stories of the great battles that raged on the plains. They told stories of how Pahokatawa fought for the people. It was Pahokatawa who warned the people when enemy tribes invaded Pawnee territory, and it was Pahokatawa who helped them prepare to fight. It was also Pahokatawa who told the Pawnee that the meteors would come.

"Do not be afraid," Pahokatawa had told them. "Some day a large meteor in the shape of a turtle will fall on the land, and when it falls, it will cause other meteors to fall after it. They will fly through the sky and light the world, but they will not harm you."

Stories of Pahokatawa passed from earth lodge to earth lodge for many years. In these stories the great warrior fought, and in these stories he died at the hands of an enemy. The day Pahokatawa died, the people mourned. They gathered around his body and wept for the brave man who had kept them safe from harm. Nature had no mercy for Pahokatawa. The coyotes and birds ate his flesh and devoured his brain. Nothing remained of Pahokatawa but bones.

Legend has it that Pahokatawa guided and protected the Pawnee while he lived on Earth, and legend has it that the star gods guide and protect the Pawnee while they rule from the sky. The Pawnee believed that everything on Earth came from the sky, and that the gods sent down to the villages all that the people needed. The sky gods chose to save Pahokatawa and return him to the people. On a dark night as the bones of the dead warrior lay lifeless on the hilltop, Tirawahat ordered the animals to return Pahokatawa's flesh. Then he sent a feather from heaven. It floated through the air and landed in Pahokatawa's skull. Endowed with the power bestowed on him by Tirawahat, the great god, Pahokatawa could now return to the village. Once again, he could guard and protect his people and save them from death and disease.

It was years later, in the month of snapping trees, when the meteors came, just as Pahokatawa had said they would. But by this time many of the people had forgotten the stories, and they had forgotten the words of the great man who calmed their fears. Stars fell from the sky in great numbers, and the people were afraid. But their chief was not afraid. He called his people together and spoke the words of the great warrior.

"Do not be afraid," the chief told his tribe. "These stars come from Tirawahat, our great spirit, and the world will not end." The people listened. Some remembered the stories. Some simply understood. On that dark, cold night the stars fell for many hours. But, comforted by what their chief had told them, the people did not flee to their earth lodges, and they did not fear that their world would end. Instead they looked through the night and watched the stars fly through the sky like birds. They fell toward the Earth. Many people tried to catch the falling stars. They knew that a wonderful thing had happened.

That night the stars fell from the sky but the world continued. The sun rose each morning after that and lit each day, and the Moon and stars shone brightly each night and lit the darkness. Life continued for the Pawnee people in the same way it had before the stars fell from the sky. The seasons turned, the people farmed their corn and fought their battles, and the buffalo returned to the plains each year to feed the people. After the stars fell from the sky, nothing changed.

Then one day, before the air turned cold, when the buffalo hunters set out on their long journeys to find food for the winter, something did change. As the hunters trudged over the grassy plains, they came to a smooth place where no grass grew. There they saw a stone of many colors sticking out of the ground.

"What is this strange object that has sunk into our Earth?" one of the hunters questioned. The others shook their heads. No one knew what it was. So they began to dig. The hunters dug for a long time, and finally they lifted the large stone from the ground. It had a curious shape, with protrusions that looked like legs and another that looked like a head. The hunters looked closely at the strange rock, and they saw in the stony head the imprints of eyes.

"We must take this stone turtle back to the village," said one of the hunters. The others agreed. The stone was large and heavy but the men managed to load it on the back of a pony. They carried it to their village and presented it to Chief Big-Eagle. Chief Big-Eagle knew at once what the rock was and that it was good.

"Meteor's child has come to us at last," Chief Big-Eagle told the hunters. "It is Pahokatawa, the great Skidi warrior, sent to us from the sky god. Pahokatawa will remain with us on Earth and serve as our protector."

Chief Big-Eagle called his people together and told them what had happened. He told them that the stone that fell from heaven to Earth was part of the Morning Star and that it had great powers. Then he called the village priests and made arrangements for proper worship. The priests made a special pipe and they offered smoke and tobacco to the stone. Then they put it into a medicine bundle, a bundle of sacred objects wrapped in hide that the people carry with them to keep them safe from harm. This stone they included in their Morning Star bundle. The Morning Star bundle held the protective powers of the most powerful star in the sky. Chief Big-Eagle kept the bundle with him in the village until white men came and relocated the Pawnee to Indian territory in Oklahoma. Then he carried the sacred stone to the western part of the land and placed it on a hilltop under the stars.

For as long as the sacred stone and the Morning Star bundle remained with the people, Pahokatawa, Meteor's child, protected the village. Skidi priests honored him with offerings, and Skidi warriors prayed to him before battles. No longer would falling stars frighten the Pawnee people, because as the legends tell them, Tirawahat, the great god, sends the people on Earth all that they need from his celestial home in the sky. And as the legends tell them, the stars that light their world are good and kind and have protective powers. These legends, like the legend of Pahokatawa, pass from earth lodge to earth lodge and from generation to generation, and they live on—for as long as people continue to tell them, for as long as the stars that light the night continue to fall, and for as long as Tirawahat rules the heavens and sends his children, the meteorites, down to Earth to guard and protect the people.

. . . .

The legend of "Meteor's Child" was adapted from accounts of the original legend published in *A Pawnee Mythology*, by George A. Dorsey (Washington, DC: Carnegie Institution, 1906), and in Meteors and the Native Americans, by Gary Kronk (*http://www.comets.amsmeteors.org/meteors/metlegends.html*).

THE SCIENCE OF METEORS

"Meteor's Child" is a myth that explains Pawnee perceptions of meteors and meteorites, but it is much more than that. Myths serve as records of events early people witnessed in their world, and this myth records Pawnee observations of the Leonid meteor shower of 1833. The 1833 shower is the most famous meteor "storm" in history, and Native Americans all over the country recorded this occurrence. The Pawnee legend serves the same purpose a scientific report would serve today. It helps explain the significance the Pawnee assigned to meteor showers, and it documents the Pawnee practice of meteorite worship.

It's hard to imagine what the sky looked like on a dark night in the Central Plains with no city lights obstructing the heavens, and it's hard to imagine what it was like to believe that the stars were falling from the sky. But the Pawnee were astute skywatchers. They knew the patterns of the celestial bodies and they understood more "science" than one reading of their meteor myth reveals.

BELIEF: Meteors are celestial in origin; they come from the sky.

In "Meteor's Child" meteors came from the stars. Pahokatawa was believed to be a part of Morning Star, a "star" that played a significant role as a powerful sky god in myths all over the world. In other myths from other places, meteors came from the Moon. Some native groups in California told a myth linking meteors to the Moon. They called meteors the "Moon's children." Some tribes in New Guinea also linked meteors to the Moon. In their myths a woman lived in the Moon, and a flaming light flashed across the sky when this woman flew down to Earth to capture someone to take her place.

People from cultures all over the world told myths of meteors because they appeared to come from the sky, the place where the greatest powers lived and ruled. Gods who ruled from the sky controlled the world, so anything that came from the celestial sphere had supernatural power. Most everyone considered meteors celestial phenomena. Many early myths connected meteors with the thunder gods responsible for storms. Even the groups who believed meteors came from thunder considered them celestial, however. Ancient skywatchers knew nothing of the layers of atmosphere that separated the Earth from the sky. Thunder, like starlight and moonlight, appeared to come from the heavens, so in myths the great thunder gods lived in the celestial realm with the other sky gods. When they drove their celestial chariots, the rumbling wheels made the sounds of thunder the people heard on Earth. When they hurled their celestial hammers, streaks of lightning flashed across the Earth's skies. People from Scandinavia called meteorites "thunderstones" and believed they were actual pieces of Thor's hammer. Thor, one of the most powerful gods in Norse mythology, hurled the meteorites to Earth, and later, when the people found them, they worshipped these celestial rocks and considered them souvenirs of their thunder god.

Meteorites, we know now, are fragments of rock, though it's easy to see why the Pawnee and many other people thought they were stars. When they streak through the sky as meteors, they look about the same size as stars. They're really much smaller, though. Even very large meteors are millions of times smaller than the Sun, a typical star in our galaxy, but they're much closer to Earth. Those flashes of light we see twinkling in the distance are less than 100 miles away from us, while stars are trillions of miles away.

Cultures that identified meteors with stars were incorrect, but the Pawnee believed their sacred meteorite was part of the Morning Star. Most people identified the Morning Star as the planet Venus but the Pawnee identified it as the planet Mars. Scientists later discovered that some meteorites do come from Mars. These rock fragments broke off from the planet when other rocks in space crashed into it long ago. Some meteorites broke off from comets or asteroids and others broke off from the Moon. This means that cultures that identified meteors with the Moon were correct as well. The meteorites that come from the Moon were hurled into space millions of years ago when other meteors blasted into the lunar surface.

When celestial bodies collide, the broken fragments of rock sail through space and become meteoroids. Meteoroids—not meteors—is the correct term for the rocks while they're still in space. While in space, meteoroids travel in fixed orbits around the Sun, just like the Moon and the planets travel in fixed orbits around the Sun. Then, when a meteoroid's orbit intersects with the Earth's gravitational field, the gravity pulls the meteoroid into the atmosphere where it collides with molecules in the air and burns up. The streak of glowing light we see from Earth is called the meteor—and it looks like a star falling from the sky.

BELIEF: Meteors are stars falling from the sky.

Meteors are not falling stars, but this belief was so common among early skywatchers that the term "falling star" became entrenched in our vocabulary. Even today people refer to meteors as falling stars, or sometimes as shooting stars. The belief that these strange moving objects were falling or shooting down from the heavens occurred worldwide and appeared in the myths and legends of many cultures.

Every day more than a thousand meteoroids hit the Earth's atmosphere and become meteors. Most are the size of grains of sand or specks of dust and they burn on impact when they hit the air. By the time we see meteors, the rock fragment has ignited and disappeared, and nothing "falls" from the sky at all. But in some cases, something does fall. Sometimes the rock fragments are so large or move so slowly that they survive their collision with the air. About one in 10,000,000 of them breaks through the atmosphere and falls through the sky. Scientists estimate that more than 10,000 tons of meteoroids break through the atmosphere every year, and while much of this space debris lands in the oceans, about forty tons of it land on Earth. The Pawnee and other early skywatchers knew that. When a meteor lands on Earth, it becomes a meteorite.

BELIEF: Sometimes falling stars land on earth.

There are several factors that determine whether meteors land on earth and become meteorites. One factor is size. Larger meteors have a much better chance of falling to Earth than smaller ones. Another factor is speed. In space, meteoroids travel at different speeds—the faster ones travel at about twenty-six miles per second, and the slowest ones travel at about six miles per second. If the meteoroid hits the atmosphere at too slow a speed, it survives.

While most meteoroids are smaller than pebbles, some are as large as one inch in diameter. When these break through the surface, they're called fireballs, and fireballs are unusually bright. A meteoroid the size of a fireball enters the Earth's atmosphere about once a century, and when it does, skywatchers on Earth can certainly see the explosion. Fireballs can outshine the stars and the planets, and some can even outshine the full Moon. Fireballs also make noise. Observers of fireballs have said they heard hissing, humming, or crackling sounds. Some observers have heard loud booms, like claps of thunder. If fireballs are so loud and so bright, it seems that it would be easy for observers on Earth to see where they land. But almost all meteorites—even fireballs—lose light before they hit ground. Then they simply disappear into the darkness. When people on Earth discover the meteorites that have fallen from the sky, they have in their possession an object from another world.

BELIEF: The presence of meteors indicates disorder in the heavens.

The movement of the Earth and other planets around the Sun is one obvious example of order in the heavens. But there are many other examples, and meteor showers are one of them. The Pawnee patterned their lives after the order they witnessed in the heavens. They watched the regular movements of the Sun, Moon, and stars, and they considered the patterns they witnessed rules that the sky gods established for people on Earth to follow. Stars falling from the sky appeared to defy world order, and lots of stars falling at once seemed to mean utter chaos. Early people had no idea that the meteor showers they witnessed were just as orderly as the movements of the planets. They had to learn the pattern of meteor showers, and the meteor shower the Pawnee recorded in 1833 helped them.

During most of the year and on dark nights, people who observe the sky might see five or six meteors. These occur randomly and can't be predicted, and they can flash across the sky from any direction. At certain times of the year, however, large numbers of meteors flash through the sky. Then skywatchers see many more. These are not random meteors; they follow a pattern. They occur on the same dates each year, and they all originate from the same point in the sky.

This is what the Pawnee people saw in the myth. They saw a meteor shower, the Leonid meteor shower, which occurs each year in mid-November. Meteor showers occur each year on the same dates because the meteors that fall in these showers come from comets rather than asteroids, and these meteors travel in the same orbits as the comets. They move around the Sun like the Earth and the other planets. When the orbits of comets cross the orbit of the Earth, many meteoroids get sucked into the atmosphere and explode. This looks like lots of stars falling from the sky, one after another.

It took scientists a long time to discover the facts about meteors and to learn that meteor showers follow a pattern and reflect order in the heavens. Until 1833 scientists believed that meteors were atmospheric phenomena, so it's interesting to read early myths that connect meteors to thunder gods. The Leonid storm of 1833 was amazing, and people all over the world watched it closely. The storm lasted nine hours, and over that time period observers noticed that all the meteors came from the same point in the sky. Observers also noticed that the meteors moved across the sky with the stars. Scientists realized that if the meteors moved with the stars, they could not come from the atmosphere because they weren't following the Earth's rotation. They had to come from the sky. Once scientists learned that meteors came from the sky, they connected them to celestial bodies.

The meteor shower the Pawnee documented in "Meteor's Child" was actually a meteor storm, the most spectacular meteor storm in history. When scientists studying the 1833 storm learned that intense meteor showers occur every thirty-three years, they were able to trace this particular shower to a comet—the comet Tempel-Tuttle, which travels in an elliptical orbit around the Sun and comes nearest to the Sun every thirty-three years. The closer a comet gets to the Sun, the more particles traveling with the comet get sucked into the atmosphere, and a storm of meteors flashes through the sky. During an average meteor storm, skywatchers may see fifty or sixty meteors in an hour. During the Leonid storm of 1833, some skywatchers saw as many as 10,000! People all over the world witnessed this event, and many of them thought something was terribly wrong.

Records of skywatchers from times past confirm that the Leonid shower followed a pattern, and once scientists learned that pattern they learned that other meteor showers followed the same rules. Look at Figure 7.1, which shows the origin of the Leonid meteors.

FIGURE 7.1 • The Leonid Meteors

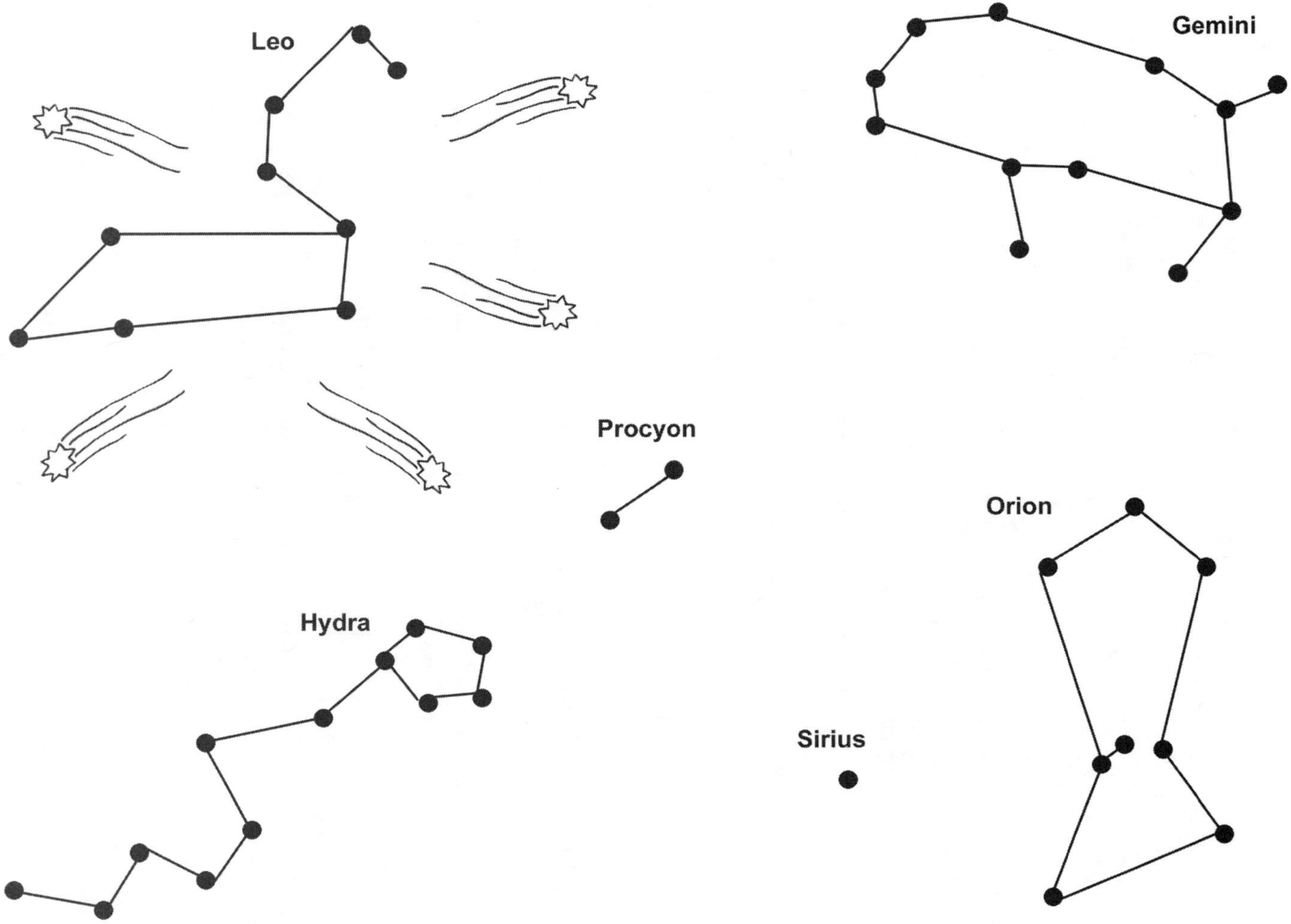

As observers watched the sky that November night in 1833, they noticed that the flashes of light came from a point somewhere within the constellation Leo. So scientists named this meteor shower Leonid, and they named the other annual showers after the constellations of their origin too. Take a look at Table 7.1, which lists the annual dates of major meteor showers. The Perseid meteor shower occurs each August and originates in the constellation Perseus. This might be the easiest one to observe today. It's warm enough in August to go outside at night, for one reason. If you have a clear, moonless sky and can get away from city lights, you have an especially good chance of seeing an impressive display of Perseids streak through the darkness.

TABLE 7.1 · Dates of Annual Meteor Showers

Meteor Shower	Date
Quadrantids	January 4
Lyrids	April 21, 22
Eta Aquarids	May 3, 4
Delta	July 25–31
Perseids	August 11
Orionids	October 21
Taurids	November 2–4
Leonids	November 17
Germinids	December 13
Ursids	December 22

BELIEF: Meteors can cause harm and may mean that the world is coming to an end.

Myths and legends all over the world reveal that ancient people thought meteors could cause harm. Some people believed them to be supernatural beings or demons with evil powers. Others believed them to be omens of death and disease, or sometimes the end of the world.

Meteors, of course, are not supernatural beings and they don't have evil powers. They are falling rocks, however, and these falling rocks have hit the Earth hard enough to make gigantic craters in the ground. There is one documented case of a meteorite hitting a person. In 1954 a meteor blasted through the roof of a house in Alabama, bounced off a radio, and hit a woman sleeping on her couch. This woman is the only person in the world known to have been hit by a meteorite, and she was left with only a badly bruised hip. In 1971 a meteor fell through the roof of a house in Connecticut, and in 1982 a meteor fell through the roof of another house in the same town. No one was hit by either of these meteors. Then in 1992, a meteor hit a Chevy Malibu in a driveway in Peekskill, New York. The car belonged to an eighteen-year-old girl who, thankfully, was not in her car at the time. She heard the crash from inside her house and ran outside to find the meteorite, still warm from its trip through the atmosphere, imbedded underneath the car. It had blasted through the trunk.

These stories are certainly unusual but rocks do fall from the sky, and often. Most of them land in the oceans, and most that fall on the Earth are too small to cause damage. But very large meteorites have crashed into the Earth and made craters on every continent. Scientists have identified about 150 meteorite craters worldwide. The United States has two very large ones. The Odessa Crater was formed over 200,000 years ago when a meteorite crashed in what is now west Texas. This meteor created a hole 530 feet in diameter and about seventy-five feet deep. Then, about 50,000 years ago, a meteorite the size of a house crashed into the Arizona desert and created what is now known as Meteor Crater. Meteor Crater measures three quarters of a mile wide and 600 feet deep, and scientists estimate that the rock that created it must have weighed one million tons.

Legends and stories all over the world indicate that people feared destruction from meteors, and many believed meteors meant death to the world. Could a meteorite be so large and so heavy that it could fall to Earth and destroy civilization? There's little chance of that in our time. Many scientists believe that one or more meteorites hit the Earth and destroyed the dinosaurs, but that was 65 million years ago, and that theory has not been proven. Most of the large craters in the world were formed long ago, in the early stages of the solar system, and most meteorites that have landed on Earth since the destruction of the dinosaurs have been the size of pebbles or smaller. Now that people know the identity of these intruders from the sky, they consider these space rocks precious finds. Some superstitions say meteorites bring luck.

Early people who believed meteorites indicated the end of the world connected them to angry sky gods. These people had yet to learn that meteorites were rocks; they thought they were fiery messengers from heaven, and they believed that if the gods sent fire from heaven they did so to punish the people on Earth. A legend from Saudi Arabia tells how God destroyed the city of Wabar to punish a wicked ruler, and he did so by sending wind and fire from the sky. The legend also tells of a mass of iron in the desert, and how an English explorer set out across the desert to find the iron that he thought might be evidence of this lost city. The explorer did not find evidence of a lost city buried under the sand, but he did find two meteorite craters, one 300 feet in diameter. The explorer also found iron fragments, one as large as twenty-five pounds, and many other small, black meteorites that local tribesmen believed were valuable pearls.

The explorer who set out across the desert of Saudi Arabia discovered the craters and meteorites by accident. Meteorite hunters set out intentionally to locate meteorites, however, and they scour areas all over the world hoping to find rocks that have fallen from the sky. Though hunters can find these rocks anywhere, they're most likely to find them imbedded in ice in the Antarctic because rock on ice can only come from the sky. Since the 1960s, 7,000 meteorites have been discovered in the Antarctic, and every day meteorite hunters search for more. One meteorite from the Antarctic came from the Moon and another came from Mars. Because these rocks formed when the Moon and Mars themselves formed, they help scientists learn the history of the solar system.

BELIEF: Meteorites have powers associated with the sky gods.

Meteorites have fascinated people for years, and though they don't have supernatural properties, they do have special qualities. They come in all shapes and sizes, some metal, some stone, and some a mixture of each. All meteorites are pieces of other worlds, and they hold the key to the mysteries of the universe. By studying the composition of meteorites scientists learn the composition of the solar system, and they get important clues that may lead them one day to discover that life existed on other planets. In "Meteor's Child" the buffalo hunters were instantly fascinated by the large, heavy meteorite that had imbedded itself in the ground, and when they returned the rock to their chief, the chief immediately knew it had power. Meteorites do have power; they have the power of sky knowledge. Early skywatchers knew that power well. It comes from observing the celestial bodies. It comes from recognizing their patterns and then using those patterns to make clocks and calendars. Sky knowledge comes from finding pieces of the Moon or the planets. These special rocks help us unravel the secrets of the universe, and they allow us to marvel at the idea of "catching a falling star" and holding it in our hands.

— TOPICS FOR DISCUSSION AND PROJECTS

TOPIC 1. Ancient Records of Astronomical Events

Storytelling was just one way ancient people documented events they witnessed in the sky. Documenting them through art was another. Discuss ancient skywatching and the ways different Native American groups recorded celestial events.

PROJECT IDEA

Have students choose one of the ways the Native Americans recorded celestial events and then create their own record using the same method.

1. Native tribes of the Southwest recorded their astronomical observations on rock. They used symbols to represent different celestial objects and events, and they etched them on stones and on cave walls. Have students paint rocks using celestial symbols used by the Native Americans, making sure to include symbols for meteors and meteor showers. The books on Indian motifs listed below will help students identify celestial symbols.

2. Some of the Pueblo tribes painted astronomical symbols on the walls of their kivas, the homes the Pueblo built on the sides of cliffs. Some of the tribes from the Central Plains painted symbols on their teepees to identify them with an astronomical legend and the protective powers of a particular sky god. Have students make a model of a kiva or teepee and illustrate it to represent meteors or meteor showers and a legend that explains them.

3. Many tribes of the Southwest decorated masks and headdresses with astronomical symbols and then wore the masks and headdresses in ceremonies where costumed dancers represented different sky gods. Have students make a papier-mâché mask or a feather headdress that represents a god associated with meteors.

SUGGESTED READING

Gates, Frieda. *North American Indian Masks: Crafts and Legends*. New York: Walker & Co., 1984.

> Contains instructions on making Indian masks and tells the legends behind them.

Harris, Rick. *Easy Field Guide to Rock Art Symbols of the Southwest*. Phoenix, AZ: Primer Publishing, 1995.

> Contains drawings of Indian rock art symbols and explanations of their use and meaning.

McNair, Peter, Bruce Grenville, and Robert Joseph. *Down from the Shimmering Sky: Masks of the Northwest Coast*. Seattle: University of Washington Press, 1998.

Contains pictures of 150 masks with descriptions of their history, use, and meaning.

McNutt, Nan. *Cedar Plank Mask: Activity Book for Ages 9–12*. Seattle: Sasquatch, 1997.

Includes games and activities relating to Native American maskmaking. Includes a teachers' guide.

Owusu, Heike, and Debbie Patterson. *Symbols of Native America*. New York: Sterling, 1999.

Contains a large collection of symbols from many different tribes and regions. Includes explanations and related legends.

Welsh, Elizabeth. *Easy Guide to Southwestern Petroglyphs*. Phoenix, AZ: Primer Publishing, 1995.

Contains drawings of Indian petroglyphs and explanations of their meaning.

TOPIC 2. Early Beliefs about Meteors and Meteorites

Myths and legends record early observations of the world and serve as a record of ancient "science" and as a chronicle of cultural beliefs and practices. Discuss how early beliefs about meteors led people to use them for different purposes, such as tools and weather charms. Then discuss how early beliefs about meteors led to the development of superstitions that some people still believe today.

PROJECT IDEA

The following beliefs are just a few of the ways people explained meteors. Have students choose one of these beliefs and write their own legend around it.

Meteors were gifts from the angels.

Meteors fell from thunderstorms.

Meteors were omens of sickness or death.

Meteors were the souls of the dead.

Meteors were the souls of shamans traveling to the afterlife.

Each person on Earth had a star in the sky, and that star fell when the person died.

Meteors were demons being chased from the Earth by angels.

Meteorites were little pieces of coal from the fires the gods burned in their celestial palaces and threw down to Earth when they got bored.

Meteors were the fire sticks of sorcerers.

SUGGESTED READING

Bruchac, Joseph. *Our Stories Remember: American Indian History, Culture and Values Through Storytelling*. Golden, CO: Fulcrum, 2003.

Contains a collection of stories that give insight into Native American history and culture.

Sipiera, Paul P. *Comets and Meteor Showers*. New York: Children's Press, 1997.

Discusses the relationship between comets and meteor showers and includes some superstitions and beliefs of comets and meteors throughout history.

TOPIC 3. Patterns and Order in the Sky

All Native American groups recognized order in the sky and used the sky to create order in their lives. The Pawnee constructed their earth lodges as models of the sky. The floor symbolized the Earth; the roof symbolized the sky; the central fire symbolized Tirawahat, the North Star, and the Pawnee Great Spirit; and the four posts supporting the roof symbolized the stars that marked the four directions—north, east, south, and west. The star of the north was identified as the Big Black Meteoritic Star, believed to rule the night and serve as a protective spirit. Discuss the different ways Native Americans imitated the patterns they recognized in the sky.

PROJECT IDEA

Have students make a model of a Pawnee earth lodge or some other type of Native American home and label each part to indicate its relationship to the sky. They can use the following sources to help them.

SUGGESTED READING

Haslam, Andrew, and Alexandra Parsons. *North American Indians: Make it Work!* Princeton, NJ: Two-Can Publishers, 2001.

> Has instructions for making tepees, masks, baskets, canoes, and other Native American arts. Includes information on history, culture, and ceremony.

Kalman, Bobbie. *Native Homes*. New York: Crabtree, 2001.

> Contains illustrations and information on the dwellings of people in numerous Native American cultures.

Williamson, Ray A. *First Houses: Native American Homes and Sacred Structures*. Boston: Houghton Mifflin, 1993.

> Discusses the significance of the homes of ten different tribes and includes related myths and legends.

TOPIC 4. Sacred Bundles

The Pawnee worshipped the stars, and they used medicine bundles to symbolize the power of the stars and their legends. Medicine bundles were collections of sacred objects tied together in a bag made of animal hide. These bundles belonged to the entire village but the chief controlled them. Because the Pawnee worshipped the Morning Star, the Morning Star bundle held particular significance and played an important role in religious ceremonies. When a member of the tribe dreamed of Morning Star and then woke to see the planet rising over the horizon, the Pawnee held the ceremony to worship this powerful star god. During this ceremony, they opened the sacred bundle to call upon the powers of the charms within it. In the myth of "Meteor's Child" the Pawnee added the meteorite to their Morning Star bundle because they believed the rock was a part of their sacred sky god. Discuss the Pawnee practice of star worship and the significance these people placed on star legends.

PROJECT IDEA

Have students make a medicine bundle full of charms that might have powers associated with meteors and with the legend "Meteor's Child." Though typical bundles included objects such as pipes, tobacco, paint, ears of corn, animal skins, and feathers, have students choose any objects they believe might represent the power of meteorites and the elements in the legend that explains them. Students should include at least six items in their bundles, and then explain what each object they chose represents and why. A dictionary of Native American symbols might help them select objects for their bundles.

SUGGESTED READING

Dorsey, George A. *A Pawnee Mythology*. Washington, DC: Carnegie Institution, 1906.

> A classic book available electronically through netLibrary, *http://www.netlibrary.com*.

Mayo, Gretchen Will. *Star Tales*. New York: Walker & Co., 1987.

———. *More Star Tales*. New York: Walker & Co., 1991.

> Two collections of Native American legends about the stars.

Monroe, Jean Guard, and Ray A. Williamson. *They Dance in the Sky: Native American Star Myths*. Boston: Houghton-Mifflin, 1987.

> Contains star legends from the Pawnee and other tribes.

Owusu, Heike, and Debbie Patterson. *Symbols of Native America*. New York: Sterling, 1999.

Contains a large collection of symbols from many different tribes and regions. Includes explanations and related legends.

TOPIC 5. Collecting and Analyzing Meteorites

The buffalo hunters in the Pawnee legend immediately recognized the rock they saw sticking out of the ground as something out of the ordinary, though they could not identify it precisely right away. Most meteorites look like regular rocks, so it's quite difficult to find a meteorite and be able to distinguish it as a rock from space. Meteorite hunters and collectors as well as scientists have learned to recognize rocks from space, however, and to analyze their properties. Discuss the hobby of meteorite collecting and detail how scientists use meteorites to unlock the secrets of the solar system.

PROJECT IDEA

Have students make models of the different kinds of meteorites. They can use various materials to create different colors and textures. They can then use their models to create a 3-D chart.

A simple chart might include general types of meteorites. Have students identify the composition and parent body for each meteorite they chose.

A more complex chart might include specific meteorites that have landed on Earth and that scientists have analyzed. For specific meteorites students should also include the size, weight, location of impact of the rocks, and where these rocks are located today.

SUGGESTED READING

Bevan, Alex, and John De Lacter. *Meteorites: A Journey through Space and Time*. Washington, DC: Smithsonian Institution Press, 2003.

> Explains why scientists value meteorites and what they can learn from analyzing their composition and understanding their falls. Includes some legends.

Carlisle, Madelyn. *Magical, Mysterious Meteorites*. Hauppauge, NY: Barron's Educational Series, 1992.

> Talks about the science of meteors and delves into the topic of collecting. Includes interesting facts, activities, and experiments.

Gallant, Roy, and Marcia Marshall. *The Day the Sky Split Apart: Investigating a Cosmic Mystery*. New York: Simon & Schuster, 1995.

> Discusses the famous Tungusta meteorite, which fell in Siberia on June 30, 1908, and destroyed hundreds of square miles of forest but was never found.

Nininger, Harvey. *Find a Falling Star*. Forest Dale, VT: Eriksson, 1972.

> The personal account of a prominent meteorite collector and a discussion of his collection and his techniques for locating meteorites. Gives practical advice for anyone interested in pursuing meteorite collecting as a hobby.

Norton, O. Richard. *Rocks from Space*. 2nd ed. Missoula, MT: Mountain Press, 1998.

> Discusses the science of collecting meteorites, talks about the pursuits of famous meteorite hunters, and gives advice on collecting, preserving, and displaying specimens.

Sparrow, Giles. *Asteroids, Comets and Meteors*. Chicago: Heinemann Library, 2001.

> Discusses all kinds of space debris, including meteor showers, storms, and fireballs.

TOPIC 6. Meteors and Poetry

Meteors and meteor showers have inspired myths and legends, but they have also inspired songs and poems. The Native Americans used songs and chants in their ceremonies, and many of these ceremonies revolved around sky objects and celestial events. The night sky has captured our attention since ancient times and it has inspired writers from all over the world to celebrate its mysteries in poetry.

PROJECT IDEA

If possible, take an opportunity to watch a meteor shower as a class. If you can't, read accounts of others who have watched one. Then have students write a poem that expresses their impressions of the event. They might start by reading other poems about the night sky or by creating a list of words they might use to describe meteor showers. They might also want to use what they learned about the impression meteor showers left on the early Americans and think of words they used to describe these "falling stars" in their myths and legends.

SUGGESTED READING

Bruchac, Joseph. *The Earth Under Sky Bear's Feet: Native American Poems of the Land.* New York: Penguin Putnam, 1998.

A collection of thirteen poems from different Native American cultures written about the phenomena of night sky, the stars, and the sky gods and spirits.

Lee, Frances. *When the Rain Sings: Poems by Young Native Americans.* New York: Simon & Schuster, 1999.

A collection of thirty-seven poems written by Native Americans ages seven to seventeen from eight tribes. Most of the poems describe art and artifacts from the Smithsonian's National Museum of the American Indian.

Yolen, Jane. *Mother Earth, Father Sky: Poems of Our Planet.* Honesdale, PA: Boyds Mill Press, 1995.

A collection of forty poems about the Earth and sky written by well-known English and American authors.

—— SUGGESTED READING FOR TEACHERS

Burke, John G. *Cosmic Debris: Meteorites in History*. Berkeley: University of California Press, 1986.

> Contains current research and historical theories about meteors as well as folk beliefs and myths. Includes legends and tales of meteorites from all over the world, discusses the superstitions people had about these objects, and gives information on the worship and ceremonial use of meteorites.

Chamberlain, Von Del. *When Stars Came Down to Earth: Cosmology of the Skidi Pawnee Indians of North America*. Los Altos, CA: Ballena Press, 1982.

Dorsey, George A. *The Pawnee Mythology*. Washington, DC: Carnegie Institution, 1906.

> A classic source available as an electronic book through netLibrary.

Williamson, Ray A. *Living the Sky: The Cosmos of the American Indian*. Norman: University of Oklahoma Press, 1984.

> Discusses the sky knowledge of the Native Americans and includes information on the observations, relics, and practices of various groups.

Williamson, Ray A., and Claire R. Farrer. *Earth & Sky: Visions of the Cosmos in Native American Folklore*. Albuquerque: University of New Mexico Press, 1992.

> Contains Native American star lore compiled by folklorists and astronomers.

8 ⋯⋯⋯⋯⋯⋯⋯⋯⋯⋯⋯⋯⋯ Eclipses

THE MYTHS OF ECLIPSES

Eclipses of the Sun and the Moon were two of the most frightening events ancient people witnessed. During a lunar eclipse, they watched a dark shadow move silently over the Moon and change it to an eerie red color. During a solar eclipse they watched their Sun disappear, and with it, the light that ensured survival of their world. Ancient sky-watchers observing an eclipse of the Sun or the Moon knew that these bright sky gods were supposed to stay in the heavens. When these gods slowly disappeared, it seemed as if something evil was attacking them, and in just a short time, that evil force seemed to devour them completely.

People of past times commonly told myths that featured some sort of sky beast taking bites out of the Sun or the Moon, and in some cases, swallowing them whole. The Maya said it was a giant serpent, or a jaguar, or an army of ants. Early people in China said it was a dragon, and the Vikings of the northern lands said it was two wolves named Skoll and Hat. Whatever beast appeared was terrifying, and people from all over the world took it upon themselves to scare away the beast and restore order to the world.

A legend from ancient China tells of two astronomers who were appointed by the emperor to watch the sky and inform him when the beast would come. That way, the emperor could organize the people to band together and make fearful noises to scare the beast and make him drop his prize. One particular legend from China shows just how fright-ened people were of eclipses and how serious they were about trying to prevent them from occurring. The two astronomers, named Hsi and Ho, failed to predict the eclipse, and the great sky dragon swallowed the Sun. The emperor was enraged and had Hsi and Ho put to death—even though the Sun returned to the sky.

The following story is set in central America, the land of the Maya, an ancient civilization that thrived during pre-Columbian times. It tells what might have happened in the land of the Maya on the night of a solar eclipse. The Maya were astute skywatchers, and like the Chinese, they too appointed people to watch the heavens and predict when eclipses would occur. Read the story below and discuss the people's fears and beliefs about eclipses. Then use The Science of Eclipses section to explain the facts about them. A list of topics for discussion and projects follows.

"THE SKY MONSTER WHO ATE THE SUN," A MYTH FROM MEXICO

It was a still, hazy day long ago, in the lush rain forests of the central Yucatan. It was a time when Mayan farmers built simple villages and lived off the land and when sky priests watched the heavens closely and knew the answers of the universe. On that day long ago, an eerie calm covered the Earth and the sky turned dark in the middle of daytime. People all over the land feared that something strange was happening in the heavens and that something sinister was lurking just beyond the horizon.

The Maya villages stretched far east of the Yucatan Peninsula into what today is Guatemala and Mexico. The farmers kept busy that day working the fields and gathering grains, and the women kept busy pounding corn into tortillas, just as they always had. But in the city of Chichén Itzá, in a building made of stairways and stone, the sky priests saw imminent danger. They had checked their calendar and seen the serpent. He had slithered through the pages and appeared with the Sun. The priests knew it was time now to deliver a message to the people. This was the day the serpent would come. In a matter of hours he would invade the sky and attack the Sun. If the people did nothing, the world would end, and the Mayan people would vanish forever. Today, the priests knew, the great sky serpent would swallow the Sun whole; he had done it before and he would do it again—unless something was done to stop him.

Priests all over the Mayan world agreed that something horrible would threaten the world that day. They knew because they knew the ways of the sky gods and they had taken care to track their movements across the heavens. But ordinary people did not know the ways of the gods and they did not understand the movements of the heavens, so they went about their business as usual. The people in the rain forests and the people in the fields knew nothing of the serpent. They knew danger when the priests warned them of danger, however, for they knew the priests understood events in the sky.

The common people may not have learned to read messages in the heavens, but they did fear the sky powers, and they did heed the advice of the priests. They saw the haze, and they heard the priests' message. Fear embraced them. The women stopped making tortillas, and the men stopped sowing the fields. The people in the fields and the people in the rain forests stopped their daily activities. An eerie calm engulfed the land. The Maya understood that this was a time to band together, to fight the chaos, to rescue the Sun, and to save the world from destruction.

None of the people in the fields or in the forests knew exactly what would happen once the priests gave their warning, but everyone imagined strange and horrible things. The people in the rain forests watched for the animals to change their behavior. The people in the fields feared that the tools they used for sowing and reaping might turn on them and attack. So everyone prepared for battle. They gathered their drums and they gathered their gourds and they banded together. They watched the sky as it grew darker and darker. Then they saw the shadow approach. In a matter of minutes a fearsome sky monster began devouring the Sun.

The people in and around the city of Chichén Itzá screamed and yelled and stomped their feet.

"The serpent has come!" the people cried in terror. "Woe to the world!"

In a panic they beat their drums and rattled their gourds. These people knew the ways of the serpent. They had seen it coil and slither ominously through the fields, and they had watched it swallow its prey whole. They watched in terror as the great snake that invaded the heavens proceeded to swallow the Sun. But the people continued to make noise. The screaming of their voices and the beating of their drums filled the Earth and joined with the sounds of other screams and other drums. All the people in the fields and the forests and in villages all over the Mayan lands joined together in battle.

Some of the people saw a large cat in the sky rather than a serpent.

"It is Poslob, the jaguar!" they cried. "He is killing the Sun!"

These people knew the ways of the jaguar. They had seen it sneak through the darkness and they had watched it stalk and kill its prey. They screamed and yelled at the monster as it attacked the Sun. But Poslob filled the sky with balls of fire, and red flames of destruction seeped through the darkness. The jaguar continued to eat the Sun and annihilate the world.

Some of the people feared an earthquake would follow the chaos in the sky.

"The evil Kisin will come out from under the Earth!" they cried. "The jaguars will come up from the ground and devour us all!"

All over the land, the Maya saw death in the heavens and feared the fate of their world. All over the land the people filled the Earth with noise. Some people saw a giant scorpion attack the Sun, and some saw a giant lizard. Others saw the souls of evil people attack, and others watched an army of ants invading the sky. Some people believed that it was the Moon that was fighting a horrible battle with the Sun, and some people knew for certain it was giant birds that attacked. The people covered their faces, deathly afraid that the birds would swoop down from the heavens and attack them too, pecking out their eyes and causing them blindness.

Everyone who listened to the sky priests knew the dangers, but the event that took place in the heavens that day was so spectacular that some people could not help but watch it. Some of the people watched the monster devour the Sun by looking at reflections of the Sun in containers of water. Others looked in reflective stones they found lying on the ground. As they watched, the sight of the monster devouring their Sun terrified the people all the more, and they screamed and stomped and pounded and banged. People throughout the land tried with all their might to scare the demon, to rescue the Sun, and to save their world.

Then, as the people struggled, the great sky monster accomplished his mission and swallowed the Sun. Darkness engulfed the land. The Earth was in grave danger and no one believed they would survive.

The sky priests had known this time would come because the sky priests who lived before them and the sky priests who lived before them took care to watch for signs in the heavens and make note of the times the demons attacked. These demons had attacked the Sun before, but more often they had attacked the Moon goddess Ix Chel and swallowed her whole. Sometimes the demons simply took a large bite out of Ix Chel and weakened her.

The priests lived in a world far removed from the peasants; and they observed the heavens from stone structures with winding staircases to the stars that allowed them access to the sky powers. Ah Kin was the sky priest of the Yucatec Maya. His name meant "he of the Sun." Ah Kin, like all Mayan sky priests, had powers far beyond the ordinary. Ah Kin had powers that allowed him to speak to the gods directly and to communicate their will to the people.

On that night, the gods did not will the world to end, however, and the people understood that when they saw the Sun emerge unscathed from the monster's mouth. Their screams turned to sounds of rejoicing. The people put down their drums and they put down their gourds. The Maya people had succeeded this time—they had scared the monster, they had rescued the Sun, and they had saved their Earth. In a short while, the bright sky god who nourished the fields and guaranteed life filled the world with light. The monster disappeared. He would return again some day; the people feared, for he had attacked before and he would attack again. Only the sky priests knew when. For now, the world would survive. The corn would grow, the land would flourish, and the Maya would continue to work the fields and pound their tortillas in the lush, green lands of the Yucatan.

. . . .

"The Sky Monster Who Ate the Sun" was created from numerous secondary sources on the culture and astronomy of the ancient Maya. Susan Milbrath's book, *Star Gods of the Maya* (Austin: University of Texas Press, 2000) was particularly useful for identifying specific eclipse monsters, beliefs, and superstitions.

THE SCIENCE OF ECLIPSES

While in much of the ancient world people watched mysterious shadows move over the Moon and the Sun and thought the world was coming to an end, most people today recognize these phenomena as eclipses. The serpent or the jaguar or the army of ants was only the Moon casting a shadow over the Earth or the Earth casting a shadow over the Moon.

The Maya may not have understood that supernatural beings and frightening sky beasts did not inhabit the heavens and cause chaos in the world, but they did understand how to monitor celestial events and determine the cycles of celestial bodies. The Maya kept track of eclipses of the Moon and the movement of the planet Venus, and they created records of their observations that baffle today's scientists with the accuracy of the mathematics and the extent of the sky knowledge. Even though the Maya recognized that the celestial bodies move in regular patterns, they had a profound fear of cataclysmic events. They believed in a series of world eras, each one created and destroyed by a natural disaster such as an earthquake, a flood, or the disaster the Maya recognized in a solar eclipse. They knew that the Sun guaranteed life and survival and that it had to remain in the sky.

BELIEF: Mayan sky priests could read the heavens and interpret messages from the gods.

The sky priests of the ancient Maya were actually astronomers, and they knew how to read the heavens because they were extremely skilled at their work. Mayan sky priests were some of the most advanced astronomers of their time, certainly the most advanced in the New World, and they excelled at mathematics and calendar making. They learned how to track the movements of the celestial bodies without telescopes and they learned how to determine the cycles needed to create calendars without instruments for calculation or measurement.

Mayan society had a rather advanced social structure, and the sky priests belonged to an elite class whom the people considered intermediaries between human beings and supernatural powers. Some of the sky priests were publicly recognized as having powers akin to the sky gods. The Yucatec priest Ah Kin did mean "he of the Sun." The Sun's pattern determined movement of the world, and the sky priests understood the pattern of the Sun and of other sky gods who moved in the heavens. These astronomer-priests knew about calendrics and they knew about rituals and myths. In the ancient world, religion and the calendar were intricately entwined. Farming cultures like the Maya relied on the cyclic patterns of the sky gods to determine planting and harvesting times and to determine the time for important agricultural rituals.

Mayan astronomy thrived in the classic age, between A.D. 200 and 900, and the astronomer-priests of that time developed amazingly accurate calendars based on the motions of the Moon and Venus. They developed an eclipse warning table based on the motions of Venus, and they used the table for warning people in plenty of time to take action and avert the sky monster before it attacked. The eclipse warning table is one of the most remarkable achievements of the Maya, and the Maya likely developed the table because they feared eclipses as omens of doom. Like comets, meteors, and other occurrences that struck the heavens at irregular times, eclipses followed no easily discernable pattern. Ancient people interpreted events like eclipses as indications of death, destruction, and supernatural ill will to the world.

BELIEF: Eclipses are strange events that indicate chaos in the universe.

Eclipses are strange only because they don't appear to follow a pattern. They occur at odd times, which to people of times past seemed to indicate chaos. The ancient Maya believed that supernatural powers set the rules of the universe, and because the Maya recognized both good and evil powers in the world, demonic sky beasts seemed likely creatures to cause the destruction. The type of beast capable of such destruction varied from place to place and often depended on what types of predatory animals populated the area. People outside the Mayan lands and all over the world blamed wolves, snakes, toads, and dragons for invading the sky and attacking the Sun. People all over the world gathered together to make noise and attempt to scare away the monster.

In the eclipse lore of the Maya, people had to prevent the eclipse monster from eating the Sun in order to save their world. They attempted to do this by screaming and pounding on drums and rattling on gourds. When the Sun reappeared in the sky, the people believed they had succeeded in scaring the monster enough to drop the Sun out of its mouth. The belief that human beings could influence the supernaturals and control their actions with proper behavior was common throughout the ancient world. People all over the world tried in various ways to restore order during eclipses. As recently as 1991 when a total eclipse was visible in much of Northern Mexico and Central America, some of the people who lived there made noises to avert the disaster!

BELIEF: Eclipses can be tracked and predicted.

There is nothing chaotic about an eclipse of the Sun or the Moon. Both of these events occur for a reason, and once they had been tracked and recorded over a period of years, it became clear that they followed a pattern. Ancient people who recorded eclipses discovered their patterns, and they learned to predict their occurrences with sophisticated calculations and tables.

The remarkable calendars of the ancient Maya allowed for predictions of lunar eclipses, and possibly for solar eclipses as well. Total eclipses are rare; in fact, most people never have an opportunity to witness one.

But the Maya considered lunar eclipses dangerous too. The sky priests used the tables they created to warn the people when the danger was imminent, but they also created the tables to help determine the pattern of the universe. Ancient people all over the world recognized patterns in the movements of the celestial bodies and felt comforted by the order of the gods. When something happened in the sky to upset the order, it frightened people. People learned the science of the universe by trying to make sense of what appeared to break the pattern and why.

An excellent example of a Mayan eclipse table appears in the Dresden Codex, one of the few documents of this highly advanced civilization that survived destruction by the Spanish conquistadors. The Codex is an intricate weaving of science and myth, and the mythical symbols that grace the pages of the Codex disturbed the Spanish missionaries. This document, and others, contained detailed tables that the Maya used to time their religious rituals and worship their gods. The missionaries wished to rid the New World of pagan gods, and in their attempts to convert the natives to Christianity, they destroyed many marvelous relics that attest to the sophistication of Mayan mathematics and astronomy.

The Dresden Codex was produced in the eleventh century, and it looks like an ancient picture book full of tables and almanacs. The Codex consists of colorful glyphs painted on deerskin, the most striking of which appear in the Venus tables and in an eclipse table that still works as an accurate calendar today. The Maya discovered that they could predict the time of eclipses by tracking the movement of the Moon, but also by tracking the movement of Venus. They didn't recognize that Venus was a planet, so they thought they were recording the movements of a powerful sky god. Because the sky priests learned to track the appearances of the planet as a way of predicting disaster in the heavens, it appeared as if the Venus god himself was sending a message to the sky priests.

Astronomers today develop tables of eclipses that appear in almanacs used by professional astronomers and by amateur skywatchers every day. In the ancient world, only the priests had access to the almanacs because sky knowledge was considered sacred knowledge and only entrusted to a select few. Today, anyone can pick up a copy of an astronomical almanac and see an eclipse table. They won't find serpents and jaguars moving through the pages, but they'll be able to tell when an eclipse of the Moon or the Sun will be visible from their area of the world.

BELIEF: During an eclipse, a monster is attempting
to devour the Sun or the Moon.

In a solar or lunar eclipse, the Sun or Moon is not being "devoured" in any sense of the word; it is simply being occluded, or covered up. It doesn't disappear out of the sky; it simply disappears from our view.

In "The Sky Monster Who Ate the Sun," the people watching the eclipse saw a shadow approach the Sun and were frightened. But it wasn't the shadow of a sky monster they saw, it was the shadow of the Moon. In a solar eclipse, the shadow of the Moon moves over the Earth and blocks the Sun's light. When this happens, people at certain places on Earth see the Sun disappear behind the Moon. The Moon covers the Sun. When it covers it completely, it's called a total solar eclipse.

In a lunar eclipse, people watching the sky again see a shadow, but this time it's the Earth's shadow they see. When the Earth moves between the Sun and the Moon, the edge of the Earth's shadow moves across the Moon and covers it. When the Earth's shadow covers the Moon completely, it's called a total lunar eclipse. Figures 8.1 and 8.2 show the positions of the Sun, Moon, and Earth in a lunar eclipse and a solar eclipse.

FIGURE 8.1 · Diagram of a Lunar Eclipse

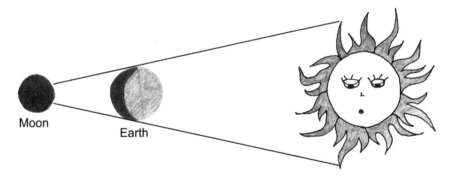

The Maya knew quite a bit of science, but they had no knowledge of the science that explained the shadow they saw approaching their Sun. In an eclipse, the people believed the shadow was an invading body—the body of a sky beast—and they believed that the beast could

FIGURE 8.2 · Diagram of a Solar Eclipse

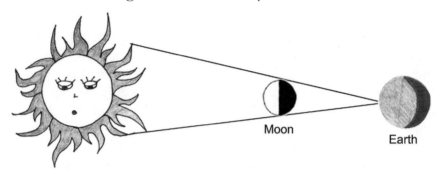

Moon

Earth

eat the Sun because they could see him taking bites out of it. The Yucatec Maya called eclipses *Chibil kin* which meant "biting of the Sun." *Chibil* means bite and *kin* means Sun. Biting the Sun refers to a partial solar eclipse, and biting the Moon refers to a partial lunar eclipse. These partial eclipses were not nearly as terrifying as total eclipses, but they were frightening nevertheless because people believed that the monster's bites left the Sun or the Moon sufficiently ill or weakened.

BELIEF: Eclipses have to do with the relative position of the Sun and the Moon.

In "The Sky Monster Who Ate the Sun" most of the people watching the eclipse believed they saw some sort of beast eating the Sun, but one group of people imagined they saw the Sun and the Moon fighting. In legend, the female Moon goddess was fighting with her husband because she was angry with him for failing to correct their children's sinful ways. This reflects a general belief that the gods punish human beings for their wickedness, a belief that appears in one form or another in religions all over the world. But the people who believed that the Sun and the Moon fought battles in the sky appeared to have some recognition that the relative position of the Sun and the Moon is what causes eclipses. The observers' location on Earth determines whether they'll see a total eclipse or a partial eclipse, and it determines who will see an eclipse at any given time.

The ancient Maya had to know quite a bit about the regular patterns of the universe before they could learn the patterns of eclipses. They had to understand the movements of the Sun and the Moon and they had to track their movements and record their cycles. When Mayan sky priests used the cycles of the Moon and of Venus to determine the patterns of eclipses, they created a functional calendar in the process. Once the Maya developed their calendar and began to record the times the giant sky serpent attacked, they learned that eclipses occur only at certain times. They learned that solar eclipses occur only when the Moon is full and that lunar eclipses occur only when the Moon is new. Today we know that eclipses involve the Sun, Moon, and the Earth. For an eclipse to occur, these three bodies must be in alignment, and that can only happen when the Moon is in either its full or its new phase.

Look at Figures 8.1 and 8.2. In a solar eclipse, the Moon is between the Sun and the Earth in the sky, and people at certain places on Earth see the Moon move in front of the Sun. Total eclipses of the Sun occur rarely, because in order for this to happen the Moon must move *directly* in front of the Sun. When it does, only people in a small area of the Earth can see it. More people see a partial eclipse, but most people on the Earth see no eclipse at all.

People who do live in the area where a total eclipse is visible see the Moon block the Sun's light because the Sun and the Moon appear to be the same size. Actually, the Moon is much smaller. The diameter of the Sun is 400 times greater than the diameter of the Moon, but the Sun is also about 400 times farther away. Therefore, to observers on Earth, the Sun and the Moon look identical in size. Proper alignment in the heavens allows the Moon to block the Sun totally.

In a lunar eclipse, the Earth, Moon, and Sun are also in alignment, but in this case the Earth is in between the Moon and the Sun. People on Earth can see the shadow of their own planet, and they can see the Moon move across the Earth's shadow. The Moon goes dark and it appears to turn a coppery shade of red as the sunlight scatters through the Earth's atmosphere. At any one location on Earth, lunar eclipses occur about twice a year.

You can see from the diagrams why an eclipse of the Sun or the Moon can only be seen on one portion of the Earth at a time; it all has to do with the relative positions of the celestial bodies. The Dresden Codex makes it clear that the Maya could predict when an eclipse would occur, but it does not make it clear that they could predict when an eclipse would be visible from their area of the world.

BELIEF: Eclipses mean death to the Sun and death
to the world.

Agricultural people feared total eclipses much more than partial eclipses, and they feared solar eclipses much more than lunar eclipses. This is because they knew the world depended on the Sun to survive. Agricultural people like the Maya relied on the Sun to nourish their crops. Death to their crops meant death to their world, and if the Sun disappeared completely, the crops and everything in existence would whither away in darkness.

Death was something the ancient Maya witnessed in their world and feared. They often saw death in their forests and fields and they simply translated their knowledge of death on Earth to death in the sky. Near Chichén Itzá rattlesnakes were abundant, and the people saw the rattlesnakes and they watched them swallow their prey whole. Jaguars roamed the Mayan lands also, and the people knew that these animals stalked their prey and ate them too. In the Mayan view, mythical snakes and mythical jaguars acted much the same way when they invaded the sky.

Death was part of the harsh world in pre-Columbian America, but it was also part of the Mayan creation myth and the story of how the current world came into existence. The idea that the world evolved though a series of creations and destructions was common throughout pre-Columbian America. People believed that each world age ended when a powerful force of nature destroyed the Sun and killed all the Earth's inhabitants. One world age ended in earthquake and another in flood, and destruction of the Sun marked the end of each world.

Some of the people in "The Sky Monster Who Ate the Sun" saw the eclipse and feared an earthquake would follow it. They spoke of Kisin coming to kick the pillars of the Earth and split it open, and they spoke of jaguars emerging from the crack and eating the people. Kisin was an evil god who lived underneath the ground and caused the earthquake that destroyed one of the worlds in the past. Some people believed that the destruction of each past world began with an eclipse. The sky monster ate the Sun; then an earthquake or a flood or another catastrophic event destroyed all the people.

In this view of the world, each world or each era was considered a Sun, and eclipses marked the change in world eras. Then, after each cataclysm, a new Sun rose in the sky. In A.D. 755 Mayan priests predicted that July 11, 1991, would begin a new era or a new Sun—the

Sixth Sun. Amazingly, a solar eclipse did occur on that date. In the Mesoamerican world view, it marked the beginning of a new world. The Sun has a remarkable ability to renew itself. It renews itself every morning after it sinks below the horizon at night, and it renews itself each time it emerges from the mouth of the sky monster and brings light and life to the world once again.

— TOPICS FOR DISCUSSION AND PROJECTS

TOPIC 1. Eclipse Monsters

Because eclipses terrified many people of the ancient world, people created eclipse monsters that embodied their greatest fears. Usually these monsters were animals of one kind or another, and the animals each culture chose were often those animals who inhabited the Earth and who posed a threat to the people in their own area of the world. In cultures all over the world serpents and snakes slithered through myths, and often they symbolized forces of nature. They also symbolized evil and chaos and threatened to disrupt the order of the world.

Discuss perceptions students might have of snakes and ask why they have those perceptions. Some people love snakes, but many people fear them. Some people fear snakes because of their venom, others because of stories they might have heard about snakes constricting people and suffocating them. Several of the books in the Suggested Reading section below talk about snakes in myth and legend, and quite likely many of the fears voiced in your classroom will have some basis in myth and legend. If a real snake can swallow a large animal whole, then why can't a mythical snake swallow the Sun whole? To ancient people, this made sense. Now take the discussion in another direction. Find out what animals other than snakes make students afraid.

PROJECT IDEA

Have students create an eclipse monster out of craft material you might have on hand in your classroom. The feathered serpent of Mayan myths represented Venus, and it is possible that this serpent, Kukulcan, attacked the Sun in some of the myths.

The following list represents a small selection of mythical beasts responsible for swallowing the Sun. Have students choose one of the following beasts or make up a beast of their own—either a real animal they might find frightening or a mythical creature of some sort, such as a dragon or a star demon. Tell them to create a demon straight from their imagination. Some of the books in the Suggested Reading list below contain myths of eclipse monsters and the havoc they can wreak in the heavens.

Mythical Eclipse Monsters

Two wolves named Skoll and Hat terrorized the Sun and the Moon in Scandinavian myths.

Rahu was the eclipse dragon of India. Rahu had the head of a dragon and the tail of a comet, and he rode in a chariot drawn by eight black horses that represented the sky.

Tzitzimime were star demons of the Aztecs who caused eclipses when they waged battles with the Sun.

A dragon invaded the sky in Chinese myths. In a lunar eclipse, the Moon turns a shade of red, and early mythmakers imagined that the Moon turned red with the demon's blood.

The Indians of Bolivia said dogs chased after the Sun and the Moon and tore the Moon's face apart with their teeth. It was the Moon's blood, these people said, that turned the Moon red. The people howled and wailed to chase the dogs away.

The Maya who thought a jaguar attacked the Sun and the Moon assigned symbolic significance to the jaguar because of its behavior and its spots. The Jaguar moved stealthily through the darkness, and its coat resembled a sky full of stars.

SUGGESTED READING

Copp, Gerry. *Great Papier-Mâché: Masks, Animals, Hats, Furniture*. London: Search Press, Ltd., 1997.

> Includes step-by-step instructions for making hats, masks, and other projects.

Levin, Freddie. *1-2-3 Draw: Mythical Creatures*. Columbus, NC: Peel Productions, 2003.

> Has instructions for drawing numerous creatures from the world's myths and legends.

Miller, Jake. *Mythical Beasts*. Happauge, NY: Barron's Educational Series, 2003.

> Contains a thirty-two-page book and and a fifty-two-card deck that shows pictures of mythical beasts such as dragons, ogres, and numerous other creatures. Has instructions for games.

Schwartz, Renée F. *Papier-Mâché*. Toronto: Kids Can Press, 2000.

> Includes eleven projects and lots of tips for making successful papier-mâché projects.

Seix, Victoria. *Creating with Papier-Mâché*. Farmington Hills, MI: Blackbirch Press, 2000.

> Contains fifteen projects and instructions for creating with paper strips and paper pulp.

TOPIC 2. Ancient Observatories of the Maya

Observatories today have computers and high-powered telescopes with which to view the heavens, but cruder observatories existed in ancient times. They stood on sacred hilltops and they graced the tops of high buildings. Ancient observatories might have been structured as elaborate temples or they might have consisted simply of ordered rocks. Ancient observatories used alignments to the Sun and the Moon and to certain stars and often served as clocks and calendars. The stone pillars of Stonehenge, the medicine wheels of the Native Americans, and the ziggurats of ancient Babylon all served as ancient observatories.

The Maya were just one of many ancient civilizations that constructed buildings from which to view the heavens, but they constructed particularly impressive buildings. In Chichén Itzá, a site near modern day Cancun, the Maya built temples to the sky powers, and they dedicated these temples to gods that moved the heavens and held a strong influence on the world.

Two of the most remarkable structures in Chichén Itzá are the Caracol and the Pyramid of Kukulcan. The Pyramid of Kukulcan (also called El Castillo or "The Castle") is dedicated to the feathered serpent that appears in the Dresden Codex, but the Maya built the pyramid about five hundred years earlier. The Pyramid of Kukulcan has stairways to the stars, and in ancient times it served as an artificial mountain. Quite likely, the sky priests climbed the stairs of the pyramid to commune with the sky powers. On the first day of spring and the first day of autumn, Kukulcan himself slithered down the stairs from the sky.

People who visit the Pyramid of Kukulcan today are amazed to see the serpent. It slithers down the stairway even now, and those who visit Chichén Itzá on the first day of spring or the first day of autumn can see him descending when the Sun sets and the Sun's shadow moves down the stairs.

The Caracol in Chichén Itzá was probably an ancient observatory too, and it also appears to have some connection to Kukulcan. The local Mayan Indians call this building "El Observatorio," but the long spiral stairway in the tower gives it the name "Caracol." In Spanish, Caracol means snail. The stairway of this building leads to a viewing chamber on the top platform where Mayan Indians long ago watched the sky.

PROJECT IDEA

Have students make a model of an ancient building, such as the Pyramid of Kukulcan or the Caracol, that might serve as an ancient observatory. People in all parts of the world constructed buildings to view the heavens. Many of them had celestial imagery on the walls and ceilings and stairways that led to the stars, and many of them had temples at the top of the stairways that allowed the priests to watch the sky and worship the gods.

SUGGESTED READING

Braman, Arlette N. *The Maya: Activities and Crafts from a Mysterious Land*. New York: John Wiley, 2003.

> Contains history, recipes, games, crafts, and other activities. Has instructions for making a Mayan pyramid and for reading and creating hieroglyphs.

Day, Nancy. *Your Travel Guide to Ancient Maya Civilization*. Minneapolis, MN: Runestone Press, 2000.

> Contains lots of photos of sites and artifacts.

Kirkpatrick, Naida. *The Maya*. Chicago: Heinemann Library, 2003.

> Covers the life and culture of the Maya and explains the work of archaeologists who study ancient civilizations.

Mysterious Places. "Tour of Chichén Itzá." *http://www.mysteriousplaces.com/mayan/TourEntrance.html.*

> Discusses the architecture and significance of buildings in Chichén Itzá, including the Caracol (El Observatorio) and the Pyramid of Kukulkan (El Castillo).

Zuravicky, Orli. *Exploring Pyramids around the World: Making Models of Geometric Solids*. New York: Powerkids Press, 2004.

> To be released in 2004.

TOPIC 3. Eclipse Table Imagery

The ancient Maya excelled at astronomy and mathematics, but they also had a sophisticated system of writing—the only system of writing of any culture in Mesoamerica. The Dresden Codex and the other three codices that survive were written in hieroglyphics, and because the Dresden Codex is the best preserved of the Mayan documents, it is one of the best artifacts that remains of pre-Columbian civilization.

When we think of hieroglyphics we think of ancient Egypt and a culture much more advanced than that of the Maya. But when scholars discovered and analyzed the books and artifacts that survived destruction by the conquistadors, they discovered just how advanced the ancient Maya really were. The eclipse table, with its pictures of the Sun god, the death god, Venus, and Ix Chel, the Moon goddess, attested to the fact that in the ancient world science and religion were intricately connected. These glyphs represented the gods who had the power to move the heavens and order the world—or the demonic beasts who had the power to disrupt the order.

PROJECT IDEA

The Dresden Codex contains numerous eclipse glyphs, and the eclipse imagery in the Codex includes the Moon goddess with one eye closed, jaguars with their heads cut off, and serpentlike creatures eating the symbol for the Sun. Some glyphs have Moon and Sun symbols represented in half light and half dark, and the eclipse table contains omens that read "woe to life," "woe to Earth," and "woe to the seed." Because lunar eclipses occur much more frequently than solar eclipses, the Dresden Codex contains many images of the Moon goddess with one eye closed eye, which represents the goddess in her death aspect.

Have students create an ancient picture book of eclipses using hieroglyphics to represent the Sun, the Moon, and the feathered serpent Kukulcan or another beast that might cause chaos in the heavens. Students can use elements from "The Sky Monster Who Ate the Sun" to create a sequence of events, and they can use the books listed below to identify pictures that appear in the Dresden Codex and that represented celestial events and sky gods and demons the Maya saw when they observed the heavens.

SUGGESTED READING

Baquedano, Elizabeth. *Aztec, Inca, and Maya*. New York: Knopf, 1993.

Includes lots of color illustrations from the Mayan codices.

Braman, Arlette N. *The Maya: Activities and Crafts from a Mysterious Land*. New York: John Wiley, 2003.

Contains history, recipes, games, crafts, and other activities. Has instructions for making a Mayan pyramid and for reading and creating hieroglyphs.

Callahan, Kevin L. "Ancient Mesoamerican Civilization." *www.angelfire.com/ca/humanorigins*.

Produced by the Department of Anthropology at the University of Minnesota, this site provides an excellent introduction to Mayan culture and astronomy with information on calendrics, myths, and religion.

Coulter, Laurie. *Secrets in Stone: All About Maya Hieroglyphs*. New York: Little, Brown, 2001.

Contains lots of photos and drawings of Mayan hieroglyphs.

Fine, Jil. *Mayan Writing in Mesoamerica*. New York: Powerkids Press, 2003.

Explores the history and development of the languages of the Maya and other people of Central America.

Michiel B. "The Maya Astronomy Page." *www.michielb.nl/maya/astro.htm*.

Maya astronomy page, with information on astronomy and calendrics for beginners.

Though not many people have an opportunity to watch a solar eclipse, some people travel to the other end of the world to see one. The sky turns dark in the middle of daytime. The world seems to be bathed in an eerie glow, and the air becomes strangely still and calm. Sometimes the animals can sense something unusual is happening and they exhibit strange behavior or stop their movements completely. Sometimes the flowers close up in darkness. A dark shadow creeps slowly toward the Moon. Then as the Moon covers the Sun, it darkens and changes color. The edges of the Sun get dimmer and redder, and the Moon becomes surrounded by a halo of light. In a total eclipse, white rays shoot out from behind the Moon, and, sometimes, jagged flames shoot out from the black rim. The red color of an eclipse comes from hydrogen gas in the chromosphere, a layer of the Sun you can only see during a solar eclipse. The white rays come from the corona, another part you can only see during an eclipse. You might also see a band of orange and red light spanning the horizon. Of course, if it rains during an eclipse, the cloudy sky will interfere with the view in the sky. You might not see the Sun very well, but you might see unusual looking rainbows!

A lunar eclipse is not quite so spectacular but it certainly is enchanting. As the Moon orbits the Earth it crosses through the Earth's shadow. When it first enters the shadow, the Moon changes color. The Earth's atmosphere acts like the lens of a camera, bending the light from the Sun around the Earth toward the Moon, and the atmosphere scatters the light and turns the Moon a coppery red color. In a lunar eclipse, the darkest part of the shadow is called the *umbra* and the fainter part of the shadow is called the *penumbra*. The umbra covers the Moon first, and the penumbra follows behind it. On a clear night, a lunar eclipse is a spectacular event, and the stars in the night sky look exceptionally bright.

PROJECT IDEA

Have students draw a picture diagram of either a solar or a lunar eclipse. They can use crayons or colored pencils and should be sure to position the Sun, the Moon, and the Earth correctly. For a lunar eclipse, they should draw the umbra, the penumbra, and the bright stars. For a solar eclipse they should draw the halo, the white rays, and the jagged flames that shoot out from behind the rim.

SUGGESTED READING

Aronson, Billy. *Eclipses: Nature's Blackouts*. New York: Scholastic, 1997.

> Contains history and science, diagrams, and photos.

Tocci, Salvatore. *Experiments with the Sun and Moon*. New York: Scholastic, 2003.

> Contains numerous experiments that explain the motions of the Sun and the Moon, and particularly of eclipses.

TOPIC 5. The Ballgame

The Maya and other groups of people in Mesoamerica played a ball-game called *tlachtli* that was both a sport and a symbolic reenactment of celestial events. The Maya constructed ballcourts near temples all over the land, and the players often wore masks of the sky gods and acted out myths that involved the Sun, the Moon, and Venus. Often in these ballgames, the Sun played against the Moon, and whoever lost the game suffered a symbolic death in the sky. There were many variations of the game and of the myths the Maya reenacted.

PROJECT IDEA

Organize a class ballgame called "Eclipse!" and play the ballgame with rules similar to kickball. Divide the class into two groups, one with players who represent the Sun and the other with players who represent the Moon. Use the books suggested below and help students make masks of the Sun and Moon to wear during the game. If the players who represent the Sun win the game, the Moon players lose and the Moon is symbolically eclipsed. If the players who represent the Moon win the game, the Sun players lose and the Sun is symbolically eclipsed.

SUGGESTED READING

Doney, Meryl. *Masks*. New York: Franklin Watts, 1997.

> Aimed at grades 4–6. Includes simple designs, color illustrations, and instructions for making masks from numerous cultures.

Mint Museum of Art. "The Sport of Life and Death: The Mesoamerican Ballgame." *http://www.ballgame.org*.

> Award winning educational site that gives a history of the Ballgame and its significance in Mesoamerican culture, provides pictures of ball courts, and includes an interactive game. The "Classroom Connection" section includes activities related to the ballgame for grades 3–12, including making masks, clay vessels, headdresses, costumes, and clay figures. Also available as a book edited by Michael Whittington, entitled *The Sport of Life and Death: The Mesoamerican Ballgame* (New York: Thames and Hudson, 2001).

Wikimedia Foundation. "Mesoamerican Ballgame." *http://en2.wikipedia.org/wiki/Mesoamerican_Ballgame*.

> Online encyclopedia article that provides a description of the game and includes links to additional facts about the ballcourts and about Mesoamerican culture.

TOPIC 6. Viewing Eclipses

In "The Serpent Who Ate the Sun," some of the people feared that giant birds were eating the Sun and would swoop down from the sky and peck out their eyes. There was a widespread superstition in early times that solar eclipses led to blindness, and, in fact, watching a solar eclipse can cause damage to your eyes unless you know how to view one properly.

Though the people in the myth were afraid of the eclipse monster, some watched him eat the Sun anyway, and they did so by watching the reflections of the eclipse in containers of water and in reflective stones. The Maya were correct to watch the reflections, and you too can watch reflections by making a pinhole camera or even by looking through the leaves of trees.

To watch a lunar eclipse you don't need any special equipment, and because they occur about twice a year, almost everyone has an opportunity to view one. Your local newspaper probably gives notice of when lunar eclipses are visible in your area, but you can also find out by calling your local radio station or by checking on one of the Web sites listed below. Once you learn the day of the eclipse and the time of maximum coverage, you can plan where you want to be during that time. Try to find a place where you have a clear view of the horizon and get as far away from city lights as possible. If you can get there early you can watch the entire show. It might last several hours from the time you first see the Earth's shadow. Look for the things you drew in your picture. Watch the Moon change colors as it enters the Earth's shadow. As the Moon passes through the shadow, look for the umbra and the penumbra. Then look at the stars and see how bright they appear.

PROJECT IDEA

Have students make an eclipse viewer, or use the book listed below to find another project or experiment that explains eclipses.

SUGGESTED READING

National Museum of Science & Industry. Eclipse 1999. *http://www.sciencemuseum. org.uk.*

Link to past exhibits to access eclipse information. Also contains instructions for making a pinhole camera to view eclipses and explains how to look at the Sun and the Moon safely during one.

Tocci, Salvatore. *Experiments with the Sun and Moon.* New York: Scholastic, 2003.

Contains numerous experiments that explain the motions of the Sun and the Moon, and particularly eclipses.

—— SUGGESTED READING FOR TEACHERS

Aveni, Anthony F. *Skywatchers of Ancient Mexico*. Austin: University of Texas Press, 1980.

> Contains a lengthy discussion of eclipse tables in the Dresden Codex.

———. *Stairways to the Stars: Skywatching in Three Great Ancient Cultures*. New York: John Wiley, 1999.

> Covers Mayan astronomy, religion, and culture, as well as the astronomy, religion, and culture of the Inca and the ancient builders of Stonehenge.

Milbrath, Susan. *Star Gods of the Maya*. Austin: University of Texas Press, 2000.

> An excellent source that provides clear explanations of Mayan astronomical myths, with an excellent bibliography.

Miller, Mary, and Karl Taube. *Gods and Symbols of Ancient Mexico and the Maya*. London: Thames and Hudson, 1993.

> Reference book that contains descriptions of all the gods and symbols of the Maya. Includes some illustrations.

Appendix: Teacher Resources

BOOKS

Andrews, Tamra. *Legends of the Earth, Sea, and Sky: An Encyclopedia of Nature Myths*. Santa Barbara, CA: ABC-CLIO, 1998.

Cavendish, Richard, ed. *Man, Myth and Magic: An Illustrated Encyclopedia of the Supernatural*. 21 vols. New York: Marshall Cavendish, 1994.

Henbest, Nigel, and Heather Couper. *DK Space Encyclopedia*. New York: DK Publishing, 1999.

Jones, Barrie. *Discovering the Solar System*. West Sussex, England: John Wiley, 1999.

Krupp, E. C. *Beyond the Blue Horizon: Myths and Legends of the Sun, Moon, Stars, and Planets*. New York: Oxford University Press, 1991.

WEB SITES

This represents only a selective list of the numerous Web sites that feature teacher resources in astronomy. Most of the sites listed contain appropriate material for students in grades 4–8, activities and experiments, and/or links to other sites for information, activities, and lesson plans.

Brooks, Susan, and Bill Byles. "Internet4classrooms." *http://www.internet4classrooms.com.*

Click on "links for K–12 teachers" to access a lengthy list of on-line sources for many areas of astronomy as well as other sciences. Has seventy-two links to astronomy Web sites.

Byrd & Block Communications Inc. "Earth & Sky Radio Series." *http://www.earthsky.com.*

Earth & Sky is a daily radio show that airs on hundreds of commercial and public radio stations nationwide. This is an excellent site for kids and teachers and it contains a wealth of science and astronomy facts, activities, and teacher resources. The site includes educational activities and classroom-ready lessons, lecture notes, and virtual experiments, as well as many links to articles and other information.

Dark Sky Institute. "An astronomy course for students using the Internet." *http://darkskyinstitute.org.*

The Dark Sky Institute's Web site on astronomy is aimed at middle school and high school students and contains a wealth of information and activities for kids and lesson plans for teachers.

Discovery Channel. "DiscoverySchool.com." *http://discoveryschool.com/.*

The section on astronomy has classroom lessons for teachers, homework help and study skills for students, and a clipart gallery.

McDonald Observatory. "StarDate Online." *http://Stardate.org/resources.*

StarDate is a radio show produced by the McDonald Observatory and the University of Texas and that airs on National Public Radio stations nationwide. The Observatory also produces StarDate Magazine and runs this Web site, which provides access to the text of StarDate Programs and has short articles and other information on all aspects of astronomy. The articles are written clearly and concisely and can be easily read by teachers and students. Click on "Teachers"; the site contains classroom activities by age level, tips for incorporating astronomy into the classroom, and information on teaching workshops offered at the McDonald Observatory in West Texas.

Griffith Observatory. *http://www.griffithobs.org.*

Click on "Star awards" to access a lengthy list of Web sites recognized for their excellence in promoting public awareness of astronomy. The list provides links to sites on all aspects of astronomy and descriptions of each site's contents.

Miles, Kathy. "Starry Skies." *http://www.starryskies.com.*

An excellent site for both teachers and students, and pertinent to all areas of solar system astronomy. Has mythology, science, and observing information. Contains myths of eighty-eight constellations and star charts for all four seasons.

The Museum of San Francisco's Exploratorium. "Observatory." *http://www.exploratorium.edu/observatory/.*

Exploratorium site on astronomy includes facts, exhibits, and teacher resources.

NASA. "Jet Propulsion Laboratory." *http://education.jpl.nasa.gov.*

> The Jet Propulsion Laboratory's Education Gateway has links to classroom activities and lesson plans on many aspects of astronomy, including comets, eclipses, Venus, sunspots, and phases of the Moon.

NASA. "NASA Kids." *http://kids.msfc.nasa.gov.*

> NASA Kids site is designed for teachers and for students aged 5–14. The Teacher Resource section provides links to numerous other NASA sites for kids.

NASA. "StarChild." *http://starchild.gsfc.nasa.gov.*

> Aimed at children in grades 5–8, NASA's StarChild Web site is written by middle school teachers and contains easy-to-understand information about the universe and the solar system, as well as activities, movies, puzzles, and quizzes.

NASA. "Thursday's Classroom." *http://www.thursdaysclassroom.com.*

> A Web site designed by NASA that contains information and ideas to help teachers integrate astronomy into the curriculum. Has weekly lesson plans and activities based on NASA news reports and recent research.

New Hampshire Public Television. "Knowledge Network." *http://www.nhptv.org/kn/cil.*

> Click on "Science" and then "Astronomy" to access The Knowledge Network Classroom Internet Library links to informative sites for teachers and students in many areas of astronomy. Includes sites on the Sun, the Moon, the stars and constellations, comets, and eclipses. Has links to many sites with pictures and interactive programs and links to lesson plans for grades K–12.

Roettger, Elizabeth. "Astronomers Education Notebook." *www.nthelp.com/eer/.*

> Produced by planetary scientist Elizabeth Roettger, this site contains lots of innovative hands-on astronomy activities for classroom use.

University of Arizona. "Educational Resources in Astronomy and Planetary Sciences." *http://ethel.as.arizona.edu/~collins/astro.*

> This site, entitled Educational Resources in Astronomy and Planetary Science, contains teacher resources and detailed instructions for demonstrations, experiments and hands-on activities.

University of Hawaii at Manoa. "Exploring Planets in the Classroom." *http://www.spacegrant.hawaii.edu/class_acts.*

> Exploring Planets in the Classroom is a public domain Web site produced by the University of Hawaii at Manoa and contains hands-on activities for classroom use.

Bibliography

In addition to the following sources, information from Web sites listed in the Teacher Resources appendix were used in preparing this guide.

Allen, Richard Hinckley. *Star Names: Their Lore and Meaning*. New York: Dover, 1963.

Andrews, Tamra. "The Caracol." *Star Date* 22, 4 (July/August 1994): 14.

———. "Harvest Moon." *Star Date* 22, 5 (1994): 14.

———. *Legends of the Earth, Sea, and Sky: An Encyclopedia of Nature Myths*. Santa Barbara, CA: ABC-CLIO, 1998.

———. "Pawnee Earth Lodges." *Star Date* 22, 3 (1994): 14.

———. "Universal Harmony and the Legend of Yin and Yang." *Star Date* 23, 4 (1995): 14.

Aveni, Anthony F. *Skywatchers of Ancient Mexico*. Austin: University of Texas Press, 1980.

———. *Stairways to the Stars: Skywatching in Three Great Ancient Cultures*. New York: Wiley, 1999.

Bauer, Brian S., and David S. Dearborn. *Astronomy and Empire in the Ancient Andes*. Austin: University of Texas Press, 1995.

Bevan, Alex, and John De Lacter. *Meteorites: A Journey Through Space and Time*. Washington, DC: Smithsonian Institution Press, 2003.

Bok, Bart Jan, and Priscilla Fairchild Bok. *The Milky Way.* Cambridge, MA: Harvard University Press, 1987.

Brueton, Diana. *Many Moons: The Myth and Magic, Fact and Fantasy of Our Nearest Heavenly Body.* New York: Prentice Hall, 1991.

Burke, John G. *Cosmic Debris: Meteorites in History.* Berkeley: University of California Press, 1982.

Carlisle, Madelyn. *Let's Investigate Magical, Mysterious Meteorites.* Hauppauge: Barron's Juveniles, 1992.

Chamberlain, Von Del. *When Stars Came Down to Earth.* Los Altos, CA: Ballena Press, 1982.

Cobo, Father Bernabé. *Inca Religion and Customs.* Translated and edited by Roland Hamilton. Austin: University of Texas Press, 1990.

Devorkin, David, ed. *Beyond Earth: Mapping the Universe.* Washington, DC: National Geographic Society, 2002.

Dorsey, George A. *A Pawnee Mythology.* Washington, DC: Carnegie Institution, 1906.

Faulkner, R. O. *The Ancient Egyptian Book of the Dead.* Edited by Carol Andrews. Austin: University of Texas Press, 1972.

Funk and Wagnall's Standard Dictionary of Folklore, Mythology and Legend. Edited by Maria Leach. New York: Harper and Row, 1972.

Gallant, Roy. *Private Lives of the Stars.* New York: Macmillan, 1986.

Gaustad, John, and Michael, Zeilik. *Astronomy: The Cosmic Perspective.* 2nd ed. New York: John Wiley, 1990.

Greimas, Algirdas J. *Of Gods and Men: Studies in Lithuanian Mythology.* Indianapolis: Indiana University Press, 1992.

Gustafson, John. *Stars, Clusters, and Galaxies.* Englewood Cliffs, NJ: Silver Burdett Press, 1993.

Hart, George. *Egyptian Myths.* Austin: University of Texas Press, 1990.

Henbest, Nigel, and Heather Couper. *DK Space Encyclopedia.* New York: DK Publishing, 1999.

Hufbauer, K. *Exploring the Sun: Solar Science Since Galileo.* Baltimore, MD: Johns Hopkins University Press, 1991.

Jones, Barrie. *Discovering the Solar System*. West Sussex, England: John Wiley, 1999.

Kaufmann, William J., III. *Universe*. New York: Freeman and Company, 1994.

Kerrod, Robin. *Stars and Galaxies*. New York: Raintree Steck-Vaughn, 2002.

Krupp, E. C. *Beyond the Blue Horizon: Myths and Legends of the Sun, Moon, Stars, and Planets*. New York: Oxford University Press, 1991.

———. "Midautumn Moon Goddess." *Sky and Telescope* 86, 3 (1993): 59–60.

———. "Moon Maids." *Griffith Observer* 52, 12 (1988): 2–15.

———. "Phases of Venus." *Griffith Observer* 56, 12 (1992): 2–18.

———. "Serpent Descending." *Griffith Observer* 46, 9 (1982): 10–20.

———. "Seven Sisters." *Griffith Observer* 55, 1 (1991): 2–16.

———. "Spilled Milk." *Griffith Observer* 57, 12 (1992): 2–18.

Leach, Marjorie. *Guide to the Gods*. Santa Barbara, CA: ABC-CLIO, 1992.

Lurie, Alison, and Monika Beisner. *The Heavenly Zoo: Legends and Tales of the Stars*. New York: Farrar, Straus and Giroux, 1996.

McDonald, Marianne. *Mythology of the Zodiac: Tales of the Constellations*. New York: Friedman/Fairfax, 2000.

———. *Tales of the Constellations: The Myths and Legends of the Night Sky*. New York: Smithmark, 1996.

Maran, Stephen P. *Astronomy for Dummies*. New York: John Wiley, 1999.

Mayo, Gretchen Will. *More Star Tales*. New York: Walker & Co., 1991.

———. *Star Tales*. New York: Walker & Co., 1987.

Mercatante, Anthony S. *Zoo of the Gods: Animals in Myth, Legend and Fable*. New York: Harper & Row, 1974.

Milbrath, Susan. *Star Gods of the Maya*. Austin: University of Texas Press, 2000.

Mitton, Jacqueline, and Simon Mitton. *The Young Oxford Book of Astronomy*. New York: Oxford University Press, Inc., 1995.

Norton, O. Richard. *Rocks from Space*. 2nd ed. Missoula, MT: Mountain Press, 1998.

Olcott, William Tyler. *Sun Lore of All Ages: A Survey of Solar Mythology, Folklore, Customs, Worship*. New York: Book Tree, 1999.

Pinch, Geraldine. *Magic in Ancient Egypt*. Austin: University of Texas Press, 1994.

Ramsey, John T., and A. Lewis Licht. *The Comet of 44 B.C. and Caesar's Funeral Games*. Atlanta, GA: Scholars Press, 1997.

Raymo, Chet. *365 Starry Nights: An Introduction to Astronomy for Every Night of the Year*. New York: Simon & Schuster, 1987.

Rey, H. A. *The Stars: A New Way to See Them*. Boston: Houghton Mifflin, 1976.

Rose, H. J. *A Handbook of Greek Mythology*. New York: E. P. Dutton, 1959.

Sipiera, Paul P. *Comets and Meteor Showers*. New York: Children's Press, 1997.

———. *Galaxies*. San Francisco: Children's Book Press, 1997.

Skurzynski, Gloria. *On Time: From Seasons to Split Seconds*. Washington, DC: National Geographic Society, 2000.

Spence, Lewis. *Myths and Legends of the Pawnees*. London: George G. Harrap, 1914. Reprint: Iola, WI: Krause, 1972.

Staal, Julius D. *The New Patterns in the Sky: Myths and Legends of the Stars*. Blacksburg, VA: MacDonald & Woodward, 1988.

Sullivan, William. *The Secret of the Incas: Myth, Astronomy, and the War Against Time*. New York: Crown, 1999.

Urton, Gary. *Animal Myths and Metaphors of South America*. Salt Lake City: University of Utah Press, 1995.

———. *At the Crossroads of Earth and Sky*. Austin: University of Texas Press, 1988.

Urton, Gary. *Inca Myths*. Austin: University of Texas Press, 1999.

Werner, Edward T. C. *Ancient Tales and Folklore of China*. London: George Harap, 1995.

Williamson, Ray A. *Living the Sky: The Cosmos of the American Indian*. Norman: University of Oklahoma Press, 1984.

Williamson, Ray A., and Claire R. Farrer. *Earth & Sky: Visions of the Cosmos in Native American Folklore*. Albuquerque: University of New Mexico Press, 1992.

Yeomans, D. *Comets—A Chronological History of Observation, Science, Myth, and Folklore*. New York: John Wiley, 1991.

Index

About the Author

TAMRA ANDREWS is a college reference librarian and a freelance writer. She has written two encyclopedias of mythology: *Legends of the Earth, Sea, and Sky: An Encyclopedia of Nature Myths* (1998), and *Nectar and Ambrosia: An Encyclopedia of Food in World Mythology* (2000). She developed a love of mythology and sky legends while working as a librarian for the McDonald Observatory at the University of Texas, Austin, and her research into astronomical legends led her to publish many radio scripts and articles for *Star Date,* a radio show and magazine produced by the McDonald Observatory. Andrews continues to contribute scripts to *Star Date* and articles and abstracts for several reference book publishers. *Wonder of the Sky* is the first in a series of four guides that teach lessons on natural phenomena through the reading of myth and legends.